I0123367

# Mindwalks

## Michael Scott

Fisher King Publishing

Mindwalks
Copyright © Michael Scott 2013
ISBN 978-1-906377-92-2

All rights reserved. No part of this
publication may be reproduced or
distributed in any form or by any means, or
stored in a database or retrieval system,
without the prior written permission of
Fisher King Publishing.

Fisher King Publishing Ltd
The Studio
Arthington Lane
Pool-in-Wharfedale
LS21 1JZ
England
www.fisherkingpublishing.co.uk

Cover image is from a painting by the
author and depicts a patio garden in which
the different plants are symbolic of people
meeting together.

# Preface

The body of the human animal is astoundingly complex. There are, for example, about one hundred trillion cells, plus one thousand trillion micro-organisms, in each of us. This micro-universe more or less behaves as a unity, which is another miracle. Most of us think, it seems, in terms of being a personal self, as if we were truly single individuals.

Each of us could, theoretically, behave as an isolated creature, grubbing around for food, maybe occasionally mating as mindlessly as we foraged and fed. We could each be a castaway on the endless ocean of meaninglessness.

Yet we seek out other human multicellulars and try to communicate. The extraordinary fact is that some communication does occur. We are even surprised to encounter diversity, as if we might expect unanimity merely because we are the same species. There is a certain degree of community achieved, sometimes aspiring to the dizzy heights of civilisation. We ought to celebrate our fragile, spasmodic, appearance of oneness.

These essays consist of explorations of the interactions between about twenty humans who are well-known to the author and who, collectively, form his mini-community of close friends. Names are invented and most of the encounters are semi-imaginary.

The essays represent a year in the author's life, focusing on occurrences that seemed epiphanic, that took the author to a new position of awareness. The book is intended as a celebration of personal relationships. These relationships may be all we have, between the reality-bubbles we choose to call 'ourselves'.

# Mindwalk

## Essays - How people interact in groups

| *Contents* | *Page* |
|---|---|

# Essay 1
# Back Then

The subject was the first memory from childhood and whether it was golden, grey or even black. Implicitly there was also the question of whether the memory was historically valid. Each person had a different picture.

The first woman, Ellen, described her moment of conversion from golden to grey. She was aged about four, seventy-eight years ago. Her mother had breezed into the room, snatched the beloved pink teddy bear from the child's arms and said, 'It's time to give this away. You've had it long enough. I shall give it to someone on the Estate'.

Ellen's life had changed at that moment, as she now remembered it. There was no way of checking the event historically. It was Ellen's world that had been shattered and stayed that way in her mind for all those decades. She felt to some degree defined by the memory-experience. It was, she said, her initiation in loss of gold.

The other people in the group endorsed the impact of such a remembered event. But when Marcus recounted his remembered loss of the gold, the group erupted.

Stefan was the one who primed the volcano. Marcus had described his remembered excitement at the birth of his sister when he was seven years old. He had an image in his mind, even now, of the baby in its cot, apparently lodged there during the seventy-three years since the actual event of her death after only ten days of life.

He then told of his agony of grief, and his memory of lying

1

on the grass in the garden, sobbing with misery. That was, Marcus thought, the moment when his gold turned to ashes.

Stefan strongly disagreed, saying that the alleged grief actually didn't belong to Marcus but was acquired from his mother's projected emotion. Stefan hadn't known Marcus at that time, of course. His strongly held opinion was based on his own life and his knowledge of psychology.

The eruption was primarily from Catherine, who was appalled that Stefan wouldn't allow Marcus his grief. She insisted that Stefan should know better than that. Marcus admitted that he couldn't say whether the remembered grief did belong to him, and had for some time doubted the validity of 'remembered' emotion.

The conflagration died down quickly and the group went on to discuss the general phenomenon of emotion in a child and the way in which it might impinge on the personality development and therefore on adult emotion and opinion. The difficulty of identifying the true memory or the actual event in childhood does seem to get glossed over in general discussions. As consciousness itself is so mysterious it is obvious that a group such as this cannot operate from a firm base. This is the background to the poem:

### Whose Grief is it, Anyway?

Childhood memories? What on earth are they,
In people who are past forty years of age or older?
Was the child in darkened room or sunlit day?
Did the flame burn strong as the air grew colder?
The more we try to think the thicker is the mist

That enfolds us as we try to remember who we were.
So why not ask the child before the chance is missed
And find the answer, just enquire from him or her:
What is golden, what is not - is not that the start?
Oh dear not, a child is so unreliable, so prone to error,
Or so it seems, there is no science of childhood thought
Apparently, and adults recoil from it in existential terror;
Perchance it does not live up to adults' rosy expectations.
Or, like a photon, changes tack when under observation.
In the quantum field of childhood there are reservations
About the value of results from laboratory examination.
We turn instead to the greater mystery, transcendence,
A perverse determination to enshrine within ancestral kind
A Sacred Thought, not drawn reluctantly from evidence
That in the human child is borne, complete within its mind

## No Entry?

Is it possible that early childhood, even enshrined in the genome, dedicates selfhood to a transcendent concept. Recent work with young children reveals deep moral attitudes and not necessarily the results of training. Very young children may be fixedly moralistic, if not necessarily the same moralism of their parents or other primary adults.

There is probably a break-point at five years, when the child changes from one kind of human being to another. The initial *Holy Idea* is not thought to change, by Enneagram theorists; but why not? And if there actually were a break at around five, the childhood 'memories' could be more unreliable as a result.

Our group has to deal with the fact that their early memories and their present emotional reactions may be illusory or at least doubtful. Who knows, after all, how a person's adult world experience is actually created? In the group it was admitted by one or two members that they regarded their own childhood memories with extreme suspicion.

Furthermore, this supposed data-bank may actually be created 'on the hoof', either at the time, as Stefan suggested, or day by day as adults, at least at the subconscious level.

This might lead us into the mind-forest in which nothing is what it seems, and could encourage us to be more reserved in our judgements and more compassionate in our actions.

The bonds of certainty and the bastions of knowledge did not receive a boost on this occasion.

# Essay 2
## Anima E-mails
(Marcus and Sarah, in another grouping)

From Marcus:

Having slept badly and late, the 'anima' question in the driving-seat, I am both less and more confused.

Thank you for your information. It confirms my understanding, which is good. And maybe something is happening to me as the model predicts. I don't **know**, of course, which is the reason for the confusion.

I have had a few more dreams, which seem to confirm the shift from animus-obsessions (Tony Blair figured in one, as a person very irritated to be contradicted) and which may confirm the need for less rational deduction in my poetry.

During the night I tried out a non-logical poem. My theme was assisted suicide. I chose a nice title: (*Please Kill Me*) and tried to explore the subject without reasoned argument. The poem became incoherent with rage and rebellion, especially directed at the 'English Inquisition' that forces us to be tortured instead of kindly released from living hell. It could be worth writing but I don't think I could do it without rational analysis creeping in.

PLEASE KILL ME

Gently, with love, no pain, no sermons, just a favour
Is all I ask, I want a moment of great joy, a taste to savour;
Save me as I saved my cat of grace, with grace, as he purred
Against my chest, held, soothed, as his pain was softly cured.

Pain is cheap and handy, I can do it for myself, DIY Defeat:
Garrotted, drowned, brain bulleted, twenty floors to concrete,
Poisoned, gassed, throat-slashed, bussed or trained, brained
Or flamed in petrol, it's all legal, self-administered, stained
With sin for some, just blood and bits of me I anticipate, grim
Exit from grim world, worst deal possible, insane, immoral, dim,
Is my irrelevant opinion, the powers be beyond me, fellow fools
Who set the rules, the English Inquisition, those po-faced tools
With thumbscrews in their souls, 'Thou shalt be tortured as God
Decrees, and so shall any man that helps thee, thou sorry sod.'

Assisted Suicide, the crime of choice for me, 'Please Kill Me'
Isn't much to ask, you'd think, said and done pleasantly.
Of course it might be murder by mistake, as the surgeons do,
But anaesthetics and good intentions make that all right too.
Nothing's perfect unless everything is perfect which it really is
So death is nothing much is it? There's a lot of it about, in this
Place of natural mess and bother, and there's them who'd tidy it
If they could, and who keep on trying, who want to do their bit
For law and order and make their views into rules, like I can't die
When and how I want to die, theoretically, and so I have to lie
And cheat my way to sweet oblivion, or travel to a killing clinic
And die the stupid death of an ignominious and foolish cynic;
What about my bloody so-called human rights, is that a scam
Like everything else on this poor earth, and do I give a damn?

Then a new thought: if I am this mixture of emotion and
reason (and how could I be otherwise?) then how and why
should I skew it away from balanced, or conflicted,

6

being/living? Taking the right/left brain theory as real, for the sake of argument (!), would I really want to kill the left side? In poetry or in living?

No, certainly I wouldn't. I'd be dead before my time. Thus my rebellious spirit claims. But is this what the anima demands: some sort of death, anyway? It can't be discounted.

So, the Fourth Instar is in process, it seems. At least one firm idea has emerged from the shifting fog: it is that it would be absurd and counterintuitive of me to **decide** to write, or live, less 'rationally', or more intuitively, or whatever. That really would be left-brain gone mad. There has to be a self-allowing process here. Maybe I just need to lift my foot on the logic-throttle. Maybe I have already started. I think my painting is well on with that.

More positively, I love the place you describe for yourself and perhaps Ellen. Your four steps are wonderfully powerful. In a curious way, there is complete equivalence between your processes and mine. And I feel that I may well be in your 4th stage, the *Dark Side of the True Self*. If so, this is poignant because of all my work on 'the Self' (viz *Mystikosmos*) in which the middle self is the Imaginative power-house, half mad, dangerous and yet productive of wonders. I have castigated it in *Mystikosmos* of course, and I think that's right. But the massive emotional force of the Imaginative Self tends to blot everything else out.

Perhaps it is really the Animus of Jung, the Personality of the Enneagram, and the Rationality of analytical thought and behaviour. So there's a can of worms.

We could start a degree course on this, couldn't we, says

the Animus.

Love. See you soon

(From Sarah): Hi Marcus

Lots of work in progress I think for both of us - it will be interesting to see where it all takes us by next week. I am fascinated to read your poem, *Please Kill Me,* written as I suggested. It is certainly emotionally direct, although there is quite a bit of reasoning in it as well.

I can certainly perceive that the animus and anima imagine a sense of death or annihilation (reducing it to a sense of nothing) but the role of the anima is to become a guide or mediator to the Self. My understanding is that you could ask the anima the meaning of your dreams in relation to the process currently in progress. How do you imagine your anima - as a beautiful young woman, a she-devil, or is it Ellen in all her beauty and majesty. If it is Ellen, then actually just by talking to her, she would automatically give you the answers as if from that part of your mind.

Also as the man takes his feelings, moods, expectations and fantasies and fixes them in poetry or painting etc then more will come up from the unconscious. My sense then is that the anima would become a very active and positive go-between from the unconscious to the conscious helping the man to translate from the conscious form to the unconscious form. These aspects would of course be both positive and negative, so writing your poem with such angst would be entirely appropriate.

I guess this initially would be like writing rubbish because it would make no logical sense, but after a while as you and the translator (anima) become more acquainted with each other and how you work, then whatever comes out will be a better and better translation?

Degree Course! Now there is a thought - how to write a degree course from such a different viewpoint - would certainly have made my life a lot easier to have done one coming from this place with tutors who understand it!

On Saturday I started with a new group of students and of course there is one guy who was a right 'pain in the arse' - knew it all and was very opinionated - again he was showing me my animus. On the way home I found my mind wandering to how I could deal with him and also win the game, because I knew I would win - you don't take me on!

I mention these examples as today I went back to looking at my notes on the animus:

The animus is right, is opinionated and very hard to contradict and full of 'oughts and judgements'.

This can fill a woman's mind with calculating thoughts of malice and intrigue (as I had for the student) and even murderous thoughts. This has to be the dark side of the True Self but this also allows the woman to see the bridge that leads to the True Self and the True Reality (whatever that is going to be).

I know for me the True Self will be to live life with Compassion, as I have said before, but a friend emailed me a lovely definition of compassion which was much more complete and mentions that compassion is also to live life with (com)passion and it feels so right for me to be living life with Passion.

The animus, however, can lead to a paralysis of feeling, a sense of nullity and insecurity and I realise that my 'peace' on Friday night at the concert was in fact paralysis of my feelings which obviously is a very old protection mechanism but one I need to learn to move through. It helps so much recognising paralysis because once released it develops into outrage and very strong negative feelings.

Women do need an animus to function in the world but in its positive aspects, but we can only connect with these once we own the murderous, malice ridden negative aspects I suspect and of course we all want to be 'nice people'.

Interestingly women with Asperger's Syndrome behave more from their animus because the Asperger's condition usually affects the right intuitive hemisphere and causes them to have opinions, not listen, talk over people, and they are unable to connect with others or see their emotions - so perfect for me to learn my lesson!

Well, no doubt you are having similar fun with your anima, Marcus!

# Essay 3
# Anna, and Others

Analysis of a note to himself from Marcus recording a mystical event at five a.m., first Wednesday in October.

*Last evening the living room was full of people, talking and meditating, until ten pm. I slept heavily and awoke at five with a single phrase in my mind: 'And how is the beautiful Anna?'*

*Odd enough in itself, as Anna is very sad about her stricken parent. I had been thinking about him and the other stricken people as well as the good souls in last evening's meeting. Maybe the dream words are not so odd, especially as so much of the group-discussion had been about our individual attempts to help the stricken world.*

*The next thing at five a.m. was that, in the darkness of the bedroom and the blackness behind my closed lids there was a sudden flare of very intense yellow colour. I have often experienced the 'yellow flower' of meditation. so-called in 'The I Ching', but this yellow colour was many times brighter, almost like an accidental look into the noonday sun.*

*The colour filled my vision, then it contracted into a single, abstract shape, even more intensely golden. My self-preservation impulse was to wonder if the recent cataract operation had gone wrong. But I didn't open my eyes, wanting to stay with the magic in my vision.*

*A few seconds later the light vanished and my eyes were*

*'normal' again. But the memory of the vision remained and I still mentally 'see' it.*

*I felt that I should tell Anna; that it might be important for her. But is it not just for me? I don't know. A mystery. I have to wait, I think. Anyway, I am in no doubt that this is one of the most potent of my mystical experiences. It feels sublimely good in my being. Maybe it is a mysterious pulse of food-energy for the changes I am experiencing. Or maybe I am just becoming senile. Feels good, either way.*

It's as if the results from the group discussing the lost 'gold of childhood' segued in Marcus's consciousness into goldenness *now,* the best time for it anyway, and there is also the fact that his eyesight and his painting have together changed to make a new, brighter clarity, and a new form within the painting

Meanwhile, he has had 'anima' dreams in which the woman-visitor is compassionate and helpful. There is no knowing what anima will do next, but Marcus walks with a lighter step today.

On a sadder note, his recent meeting with Sarah and Ellen was eerily quiet, as if Sarah had 'gone away' in some way. He described it as follows:

*We met Sarah in her new home together with her new family of cats. It was very quiet. The cats were elusive although one, uncharacteristically it seems, came to Marcus and settled down on the carpet near him. Very strange. Sarah seemed to find a new depth and wisdom in Ellen. Not surprising, considering Ellen's recent travails and her determined prevailing over them.*

*Once the interchange got going, and it took a long time, Sarah was tearful and unable to say why. It may be loneliness, though she has much going on in her life. It may be that she has given up so much of her healing and facilitating work. There is a kind of battle-fatigue, maybe, and that can't really by helped by the loss of her mother, however difficult she had been, nor by the acquisition of an excessively self-focused tenant.*

*We will meet again in two weeks and I will have to wait for more insight or information. Sarah is an important person for me, and for Ellen, which she knows. Maybe we will hear from her before the two weeks is up.*

The importance of The Now is demonstrated again, in that the good interchange in a group on one occasion may be followed by zilch on a later occasion. It is the way of consciousness in all its abstruse nature.

Somehow very significant in the meeting with Sarah is the fact that Ellen demonstrated the unknowability of animus by showing Sarah an article from the Guardian in which the attitudes of our soldiers in Afghanistan were revealed. They love to fight and to kill, apparently, and enjoy being shot at. They say this fighting is 'better than sex'.

Sarah, struggling with animus as she is, did not particularly react to this. But were the later tears possibly connected?

### Such an Idyll

Some encounters seem blessed with uncomplicated

sweetness: as in the meeting between Ellen and Marcus with their younger friends Lisa and Paul in their quiet home in the country. This quartet has a long history. The relationship has passed through many phases. Now it is gentle, loving and almost like a close and devoted family group in which Ellen and Marcus are the aging parents.

Staying with this fantasy, it's as if the 'parents' have matured through their five years of illness and so the 'daughter' and her husband have been increasingly drawn to the older couple. At this meeting, the first for months in the home of the younger couple, the atmosphere was both elegiac and light-hearted. The core-issue was the continuing resettlement of Marcus and Ellen in a new home and the work involved in moving possessions from the old home to the new. The enthusiastic help from the younger couple was a great comfort to the older one. And while this is hardly unusual or atypical in a good relationship, the mood of Ellen and Marcus was suddenly more radiant as a result of the affection.

It is commonly assumed that old people are neglected in this society, but as they enter their eighties, after considerable physical trauma, Ellen and Marcus have been given kind attention by many people. They have a number of connections which help to sustain them - almost a caring network, though not as formal or specific as that. This, together with the friendship of Paul and Lisa, makes the prospect of their remaining time much less arid and frightening.

Furthermore, there is reason to re-examine assumptions held throughout a long life. Both Marcus and Ellen are 'achievers', people determined to make something of their lives, to grow and develop themselves. It is hard for such a mind-set to deal with 'decline and fall'. So, following this meeting with Lisa and Paul, also considering all the other kindness from friends, what adjustment is appropriate?

A key feature of their self-awareness is their aloneness. While some old people have an extended family, there is none for Marcus and Paul; they have only each other, or can think that, which makes their closing years particularly hard. But how far is this attitude just that, an attitude. And even without such a circle of friends, what is so fearsome about the ending of a life? Is something missing in the consciousness of one's frailty and approaching demise?

Marcus and Ellen do not have a belief-system offering any form of post-mortem survival. They have years of experience of energies which defy mundane rationality. Both have had many 'mystical experiences', some of these having post-mortem implications. But they accept that death is a form of absolute ending. They do have a perception of 'soul', but this seems to them to be as vast as the idea of consciousness, and just about as unknowable. For them, the refusal of a belief in personal gods or reincarnation or resurrection, is no barrier to a spiritual state of being. This is not a new horizon, as spiritual philosophers have shown over the centuries. But to live in the modern world, these ancient states of awareness seem somehow side-lined by religions and militant nihilism.

There is more to life and death than is generally supposed, for these two people, and for whom systems of belief seem to suffer from a fundamental lack of knowledge. It may be the highest wisdom to admit that we do not know. That not-knowing may be far more important than anything else, perhaps the ultimate paradox is that not-knowing is the only absolute truth.

Ellen and Marcus imagine a fine and wavy line between not knowing and not being informed. While *knowledge* of the existential variety is impossible and the very idea is absurd, *information* within understood limits is vital for a civilised life. Their existence depends on their ability to live in the reality of the actual moment, the way it looks and feels, unfettered by beliefs engendered by supposed knowledge. It is a difficult venture. Yet it holds the possibility of happiness.

Lisa and Paul seem to lean towards the same ideal, though being in their early fifties and needing to earn their living, within social and cultural orthodoxy, their task is also difficult in its own way. While they do not yet face the personal void of death, they have as much of a struggle confronting the exigencies of life. Here again, however, living in the present moment, mindful of useful information, is vastly superior to the impossible absolutes of presumed knowledge.

Thus it has been possible to meet with Lisa and Paul, whereas sharing 'the dream' with Anna seems impossible as she is embedded in an intractable belief-system, in which absolute knowledge is imposed upon her. It would be a crime to try to dislodge this knowledge. Marcus's brilliant golden light is not knowledge, merely an experience that fills him with joy. It cannot be given to someone else. Or even offered. It is not a commodity, not a piece of knowledge, but at best a flying fragment of information that owns itself.

# Essay 4
# Wandering Eyes

The word is, perhaps: promiscuity - if it means merely a muddled mixing of things, including sex and love. The starting point in this essay is the life and character of Diana Athill and the strength, apparently, of her animus. She is monumental in many ways, and has only been encountered by Ellen, Marcus and the others, in a TV documentary by Alan Yentob, or in her books.

There also a connection with a meeting between Stefan, Catherine, Julia, Ellen and Marcus, in which there was strident expression of feminine outrage at male behaviour. While not unusual in group interactions, in this case it was specific to the promiscuity of partners, especially male partners, and the ways in which the female psyche tried to deal with it.

Another thread in the skein of the essay is Sarah's battle with animus. For example, a recent statement by her includes the following, referring to another female acquaintance, V:

*'I know full well that my irritation with V is only because she is showing me my animus and how it behaves but on Monday it became clear suddenly that she is 'acting out' my animus for me and showing me my 'sacred beliefs and convictions' that I have been trying to access. Big relief for me to finally get that bit inside - my conscious mind knows it, but there always tends to be a sort of 'clunk click' inside and then things subside! My beliefs that are, as it were 'written in*

*stone' - many of which I have been working on and letting go of for years now, but had never seen them as 'written in stone' in this way. So, for example, when she insists on telling me or anyone what they should do, that is how my animus behaves and thinks it is necessary to do so. I am very aware how much of my life has been spent telling people what to do... and nowadays I catch myself so that I don't do it, but this animus is functioning at such a deep level, that although I consciously stop, that does not sort out the issue... I need another way to behave. So, the other evening someone was telling me about their niece and something this niece was doing and instead of going into a conversation about it I just said, 'well, that seems very strange to me, but then it is none of my business how she lives her life', and let it go. Big relief for me that felt so much better!*

*Anyway I must be making progress as I had a dream last night about this lovely man and in the dream I realise he is my animus... the dream goes on, but the next bit I remember is being in a bus and he is sitting with V (as if they are together) and V has a baby in her arms. So the various aspects of my animus have given birth which thinking about it feels very positive because as the woman addresses her animus it is supposed to in effect 'give birth' to new things released from her unconscious! I wait to see what they might be.*

'Returning to Diana Athill', an excerpt from a piece about her on the net:

*Diana Athill's life has been full of unexpected twists. There was the broken relationship that led to a brilliant career in publishing, working with some of the world's most esteemed writers, and being regularly described as 'the finest editor in London'. At the same time she was engaged in a maze of love affairs that saw her cast more than once as 'the other woman'. And now, at 91, when most people's lives have slowed down considerably, Athill is enjoying perhaps her most exciting and unexpected new chapter - winning huge critical and commercial success as a writer.*

*Her latest memoir, 'Somewhere Towards the End', is shortlisted in the biography category for the Costa book awards (formerly the Whitbread); the category winner will be announced tomorrow. She says that she is very pleased about the shortlisting, "but I'm not allowing myself to get excited". In her five decades as an editor, Athill recalls having to "sit with authors of mine who had been shortlisted for prizes at those wretched dinners, saying, 'Now, we mustn't hope, we might easily not win', and then seeing their poor faces when in fact they didn't, and they were bravely pinning on a smile." Much better, she suspects, to let your feelings show. Athill is a stickler for directness.*

It is hard to know whether Jung's inventions actually relate to anything real in the psyche or anywhere else. But when these three encounters are allowed to connect, there seems to be a definite presence in them that could well be the animus. In all of them there is strong female energy, a remorseless, pursuing force that aims, apparently, to overcome or break down obstacles. It is often sexually manifested. Athill pursued men and admitted (or claimed) to develop a taste for 'black men' and she was obviously promiscuous in the non-pejorative sense. Catherine and Julia are still engaging with their male 'targets' in different ways. And their lives are greatly influenced by their past or present men. Sarah has virtually given up men, as a hopeless venture, and pursues animus internally, as part of her own search for integration.

As the man who regards all these women as important in his life, Marcus tries to comprehend what is going on. He has enough problems with his so-called *anima*, if that is what it is, and it might be thought that he'd be better concentrating on that. But he feels that the two archetypal forces need to be addressed as a pair.

Why? It is probably because he is aware that in himself there is an active female element partnering or opposing a male element, or it may be right brain versus left. Just as Sarah, instead of hounding the male renegade, tries to pin down her animus, Marcus attempts to pin down his anima. He spends as much time talking with women as with men, and he free-ranges over territory he barely comprehends because he refuses to settle for the he-man stereotype.

A positive result of this work is that it can be seen that sexuality is not as important as it is said to be. It is important, of course, but in the same way as alcohol, amphetamines or egotism. Beyond sex and sexuality there is human consciousness, with or without gender applications. Sarah's animus is now helping her individuate, Marcus's anima is doing the same for him - as she has for many decades.

On the other hand, Catherine and Julia are still battling with the male outside as well as the animus within. They are hot-tempered, or passionate, in these encounters. Who is to say which way is the better? Presumably, awareness is all, so that no-one gets caught in a compromising painted-in corner.

As for Diana Athill, she is undoubtedly magnificent. But she seems cold and withdrawn into a self-regarding redoubt. Not knowing her doesn't help the understanding, but as she approaches death with stoicism and more that a touch of nihilism, is it appropriate to ask where love went in the engagement with the animus? Putting it another way, has she loved men, or women, with animus-driven zest, or has she surrendered to the state of being in which love is like a sea, enveloping everything?

# Essay 5
# Exclusion

A different gathering: Ellen, Delia and Marcus. They are long-term friends. They know each other well, even too well, insofar as it is a temptation to assume too much from long association.

There are difficulties in the relationship, not least the twenty-year gap between Delia's age and that of the couple. Also, Ellen is on a different life trajectory, in that she is deeply fatigued by ill-health and has left many of her activities discarded into the unforgiving past. The other two have dropped a lot of baggage too, which gives the trio a degree of compatibility. Marcus has much of his time and energy used up by caring for Ellen, while she may become insecure and bored. Delia is pursuing a lonely path but still dedicates herself passionately to important ventures.

As for the animus, there is no shortage in either of the women. Ellen is formidably intelligent, as is Delia, and is used to controlling her destiny and having significant impact on those she chooses to love. Delia, reciprocates those feelings, but otherwise seems eremitic in her tendency, which parallels Ellen's insularity in most aspects of her life.

None of these qualities are a cause of relief or regret, but misunderstandings arise in the intense interchanges between the three, especially in certain well-defined areas. Because the intensity often takes the three people beyond ordinary conversation, they sometimes reflect together on the psychological foundations of their different natures.

Exclusion and low self-esteem are important vectors for them. Even though they are well past the agonies of the mid-life crisis, that doesn't mean that they don't suffer from weaknesses they'd prefer to be without.

Aspirations abound in this trio, despite two of them being in their early eighties. They all have creative tendencies. Writing, painting, energy-based healing and transformation, and psychology-cum-philosophy are all keenly followed. However, two of the three, Delia and Marcus, are nature-mystics, and this can be a problem, especially considering that all three like to be centre-stage if they can get there and hold the space.

Ellen finds the endless interchange between the other two sometimes exasperating. The nature-mystic bond seems to her to control the relationship of the trio, even when nature isn't specifically involved. It is as if Marcus and Delia have a special connection that keeps Ellen out of the light.

For three people with such noble tendencies, it is sad for them to recognise an unnecessary friction. But it would be sadder if they didn't. Better by far to see it as a growth-area, even if all three have had a plethora of those. The question for them is how to move forward, if that direction exists, or how to celebrate the fixed point if it is the only option. One thing is certain, it is not the fault of any one of the three. On the contrary, it is food and drink for the hovering anima and animus, or whichever archetype, spirit or wingless angel it may be.

For the truth is that these three innocent creatures love each other with some passion. Not that mere love will solve anything. Some thought may also be required. Possible even a dash of imagination. A soupcon of compassion, maybe.

Further meetings may provide further understanding. At least there is dawning awareness, late in the day, but probably not too late. For the time being, there must be an intention, possibly even a contract, to the effect that further incidence of exclusion will not be permitted.

## Terms of Inclusion

She is a perfect picture of charm and cosmic dismay
And maybe that is as it always was for her, underneath
Serenity, steadiness, the sureness of touch and mood.
There is a catastrophe in there somewhere, hiding its face.
An arid family way back, the unjoyful years of work, not
So unusual, we all make do with what we choose. And then:
She burst into flower, lived a new delight, found her way.
At her zenith, in her beauty, in her power, there it was:
She discovered the inner grail, the secret, ubiquitous energy
Joining her to the other, whoever, with transformational force,
And her true tribe, true leader, true vocation, true bliss.
How could this have faltered? What dark angel drew a sword
That cut the umbilicus, killed the child before it could fully grow?
Deaths did not help, her leader lost, nor the jealous scepticism
Of her struggling mate; yet it seemed an inner doubt, as if
It was really all too good to be what she needed it to be, a truth.
That is, a truth too great to be sure of, an untrusworthy yearning
For an everything she could not quite believe. And so she fell.
And fell again. Tripping, slipping, shaking, breaking her body,
Breaking maybe her heart. Or because her heart was breaking.

Her paintings are there for all to see, her books for all to read,
Did her munificence drain that flow of shining energy, or did she
Sink into the quicksands of doubt, as now it seems, her fateful
Animus hating her unwellness, her weakness, her dependence,
Her loss of interests, her boredom, wistfulness, and what thing
It was that laid her out, and this incessant flatness of feeling.
The time is now, now the time, for her to make a new embrace:
All is still in her, spirit, compassion, empathy, refusal to be
Bamboozled, dislike of tawdriness, of sleaze, and of unkindness.
She almost sees her shame and guilt are unwarranted, and that she
Wastes time just holding on, and she must know she is now ready
For the leap into comprehension, where her trust still waits for her.

## Essay 6
## Metamind Epiphany

It happened as Marcus processed the interaction with Delia and Ellen, and reviewed these essays with Ellen.

Something very major was happening to him. His mind went back to his first novel, nearly twenty years before, in which he had tentatively explored what he had come to recognise as the third self. In the recent period he had developed his idea into a rejection of traditional self-concepts and substituted a trinity of selves, first the basic, solid, animal self; second, the immense and essentially unstable imaginative self; and third, the unknown, transpersonal, self.

In that first novel, *The Halcyon's Nest,* the three selves are blurred together and this is the substance of the novel. What has now happened is that the clarification that resolved selfhood into three forms or phases, has again altered. This time the entire self-system appears as a continuum rather than a trinity.

Not such a big change, perhaps. But included in the development is a new appreciation of the nature of the transpersonal self.

The trigger for the change was the exclusion-experience of Ellen and the struggle to comprehend between the two 'nature-mystics', Delia and Marcus. This 'exclusion' was a key issue. The truth is that Ellen is as much a mystic as the other two, maybe more so. But her mysticism is not nature - based, in the way that it is for Delia and Marcus. She dwells in a world of energy - forms and she truly detests nature for its violence and waste. How could she share in a nature-worshipping cult? Ellen enjoys the meditations and rituals of Druidry, for example, but draws the line at the deification of trees. Yet she cannot abide the felling of trees.

To complicate matters further, Marcus became aware that his 'nature-worship' differed fundamentally from Delia's. Like Ellen, he hates the death and conflict endemic in nature, yet is euphoric about natural beauty. In a nutshell, the three people are in different segments of the transpersonal, so different that they are separated by the difference. Indeed, the separation may be vital to their individual personalities.

## The Epiphany

For Marcus, an atheist, it is obviously not the Christian Epiphany, even if it has a similar force for him. He has experienced a sudden realisation of great magnitude - for him, anyway. The nature of the 'awakening' in him is that the entire matrix of imaginative and transpersonal selfhoods is suddenly seen as a continuum and an absolute mystery.

Until now, his developing awareness has included mystical experience alongside rational analysis. The division has long been uncomfortable but he has needed the stability afforded by reason.

The trouble with this duality is that Marcus has continued to be judgemental, using his reason to distinguish 'false' imagination from 'genuine' imagination. He has been trying to have his cake and eat it. Like Sarah, jousting with her animus, Marcus has been in perpetual conflict with his scepticism, perhaps his particular form of animus.

Consequently, Marcus rages against religions which have gods and embraces the few that don't. He denounces alternative therapies because they are unproven by rigorous testing. His own 'mystical' life, which is intense and fruitful, he regards with some suspicion. Theories or beliefs regarding past and future lives, of cosmic consciousness, of astrophysics, he handles with tongs.

All this has suddenly appeared to him as nonsense. It is as if the Void has not yet finished its work on him. He thought he had passed beyond the trap of knowledge and the prison of spiritual pride, but he now finds himself evicted anew from the edifice he had so diligently built.

To be fair to him, he suspected that something catastrophic was coming his way. But he could not have imagined the extent to which the 'desert of freedom' would engulf him.

He knows and loves a number of co-inhabitants of the 'transpersonal' and he has battled with them to 'make his point'. They will not know that he has recanted so dramatically. But he still has to get used to it himself. After years of denying that such a thing as knowledge exists he now has to live that fact.

### Metamind.

This is Marcus's neologism with which he now intends to describe and understand his continuum. It includes everything beyond the incontestably mundane. In the metamind there is no certainty and no knowledge. But it is the realm of everything that matters. Now Marcus has to live in his metamind unless and until he has another epiphany. It is a world of personal freedom and perfect isolation. It is as full of love and beauty as it harbours terror and despair.

## Delia's Gift from the Metamind
### Wild Geese

You do not have to be good.
You do not have to walk on your knees.
For a hundred miles through the desert, repenting.
You only have to let the soft animal
of your body love what it loves.
Tell me about your despair and I will tell you mine.
Meanwhile the world goes on.
Meanwhile the sun and the clear pebbles
of the rain are moving across the landscapes,
over the prairies and the deep trees,
the mountains and the rivers.
Meanwhile the wild geese, high in the clean blue air,
are heading home again.
Whoever you are, no matter how lonely,
the world offers itself to your imagination,
calls to you like the wild geese,
harsh and exciting - over and over
announcing your place in the family of things.

Mary Oliver

## Essay 7
## Near Death Experience
In the form of three poems

1) First Man, Adam, in his sixties, seriously ill with bowel cancer.

2) First Woman, Eve, wife and nurse of First Man.

3) Second Man, Marcus, friend of both

**The First Man**

He had been as close to Death as any of us and even closer;
And on his thin face and in his brilliant but hollow eyes
That moment still shone upon him with supernatural light.
A 'bag of bones' he called himself, a man who was never fat,
It seemed as if they'd taken too much away from him and left
Us with a wraith, yet he was full of spirit now, as if born anew.
'The scan and blood-test gave good news', he said, and he saw
That there were days to come for him to live again, leaving
Old enthusiasms behind, shedding unwanted burdens, growing
Into full acceptance of his fate and nature. 'Illness makes newness
Out of despair', he seemed to say, however sad he looked. Tears Fell
from his bright eyes, looking at his love, his nurse, his strength
When he had been too weak to stand, and now he was nearly strong
Again, but not yet strong enough for chemotherapy, holiday instead
Then, weeks in the sun, letting his body heal as much as it could.
But in the quiet room, among the tea-cups, Death still hovered
Reluctant to let the tall man go his own way, at least for now.
Death was there for all of us, lingering, which of us was it to be?
It seemed to mock us all, as if love was admittedly amongst us

Yet, whether cosmically endemic or not, love was as vagrant
As any other thing, beautiful but never constant or guaranteed;
And the tall, weak, strong man, haunted by abandonment,
But resolute and accepting of all things, stands his shifting ground:
He is determined to survive, in some degree or form, surrendered.

**The First Woman**

She comes complaining of impatience, ironical word,
Considering her absorption with the patient, her man,
Sitting nervously and wanly opposite her, but defiant.
She always gives more than is needed, her need to give
Defines her being, making her beautiful and tiresome
Sometimes because she is more than her giving, better
Than just being good, and she knows that, tries to survive
Her good giving, which makes her impatient, her karma.
Her man may live or die, who knows, but as he rallies
Against the destroying flesh, she rails against her own
Obsession, loving him as she does, risking self-exclusion.
She fears her drive to give, as if it is the kiss of death itself;
Weeks have passed in which her command of his condition
Made her strong, gave her glory, this was her great vocation.
And it has always been her bliss, a giving that made her powerful.
And made her feel a loving throb within her being, while it
Lasted, but it always had to find an end, like a defeat, or failure,
And this has always been the test: to survive declining need.
Exhaustion and anxiety etch her features, but not just this pain;
She knows her work is cut out in jagged shape, a giant predator,
It has to be now, the time to find the true need within herself:

Not, oh not, the need to give, for that is in her every cell, Oh no,
This need is transcendental, the need to face her deepest spirit
Confront the polymorphous monster-genius that rules within
Maybe thrust excalibur into its breast, maybe marry it, anything
That puts it in its place, in her power, not her in its embrace.
This takes courage as it seems to be a death, of self not other,
But it is a death that must be dealt, a killing of false significance
That otherwise will take her to its grave. But this she knows and
Will not will it, fearing lost delight, not trusting in the safety
Of surrender, the real giving, the laying down of self in peace,
Not a death, nor a sleep, but rather a long and lovely vacation.

## The Second Man

Sitting near his boar of bronze, and hugging his newest epiphany,
He had entered the Metamind Continuity wherein to contemplate
Meaning and destiny, as if such strange things actually exist. This
Old old Man did not play nick-nack, but perhaps came rolling home:
Upon a chariot of sparkling confusion, driving towards the fabric
Stretched across the entrance to reality, sharp-scything an opening
To that other world, a temporary vision and inspiration; momentarily
Seeing the terrors of the fancies, as he saw them, of the first woman
And the other man. No certainty. No eyes assured. Only a moving vision
Enclosing the other two, and all else, in the bronzeboar's embrace.
Mother Nature is Mother Birth and Mother Death, two for one, a deal
Made in hell, if anywhere, and they are hard to tell apart, because
They easily become each other, and catch us napping, hoping, trusting.
This new Old Man nick-nacked thumb, shoe, knee, door, hive, and sticks,
And up in heaven, on my gate, my spine, then did it all again, tricks

Learned in Mother Birth's nursery, with paddy whacks and dog's bones.
This was the story to tell the other two: that it is all just that, a story.
No-one likes to feel that they've been *had*, but *had* they've surely been;
Mother Birth composes, Mother Death disposes, sounds important,
Sound the trumpet, bang the drum, tell each other that we are The One,
And Only One who counts on little Earth, all of us are One, One and All, we
Love the Cosmic Joke, tell the children, sing the songs, listen all around.
The penny may fall. What if it really is a joke? What is a joke? Are we
Jokes within a joke? Minor jests within the shaggy dachsund? Is it
True that nothing really matters, as the joke goes? No, very untrue, truly:
We have ourselves and each other and dogs and cats and violets and sky;
We have ours and everything has us. Joined at hip and whalebone arch.
Tell Mother Nature, and her minions, Birth and Death, we're not impressed,
Even if they rule us they are not separate from us, for they are our bodies
And we are their souls. This incestuous love affair, and bloody bar fight,
Is not the main attraction. We have the freedom to deny our chains, we need
Not waste ourselves on fear and hope. Old Man's friends: send the ghosts away.

# Essay 8
# Quincunx Group Connections

We met as usual, on the first Thursday of the month. This time it was just after Samhain, so it might be said that the between-worlds connection was at maximum aperture. Whatever the reason, the group closed in on itself, put out the light and told their individual stories.

It appeared that each person was experiencing similar change. New, or different, awareness was happening. It was possible that the furore in the world of finance and the Greek tragi-comedy were affecting them, but each member spoke of good feelings about the future. The main thing was that the meeting was warm and consoling. It is hard to know why this group finds it so rewarding to meet, with no particular objective, but it may be that it is an exceptionally 'safe' environment, and that each member feels strong connections to the others.

All the more surprising, then, Marcus should find himself in an extreme state of disconnection on the following morning - even to the extent of not wanting to get up and face his day. It was not, he thought, the result of the group meeting, not in any negative way at all. Maybe the closeness had made him see more clearly how unclose he was to most people. He remembered how Ellen had complained of his increased silence, his uncharacteristic lack of conversation in their partnership. There may have been a correlation to his new feeling of disconnection from the world. The feeling was strong enough to seem particularly significant and so Marcus

tried to express it in his favourite form, a poem, hoping some
clarity might come to him.

## Attachment

Perhaps it has been a long preparation
For the birth of this strange separation,
The non-connection that suddenly assails
At dawn on a November day, and pales
The world into insignificance in his eyes
Until the light inside him dims then dies.
There are the day's activities mockingly
It seems, saying how pathetic it is to be
A man in a clockwork dream, ticking
His few days away, blindly picking
A path between the weeds and stones
Carrying his bag of skin and bones.

He *thinks*, as always in emergency,
To *find* a better place, where he can be
That ideal rejoicing self from earlier life
Brought up to date, with pruning knife
*Take* out old wood, *reveal* the glow
of newness, let the life-force flow.
Not this time, old man, if it ever did,
Remember what is now, the empty bid,
The null, the void, the hungry apple-core
With poisoned seeds, there is no more:
He has waited for this time, even needed
It's cold freedom, now he has succeeded.

It's not as he'd imagined it, not that he could;
He has lost a mandate, self-imposed, he should
Have realised the emptiness would include all
Including his right and duty, the divine call
To lead himself and others to a pure domain:
Pilgrims bound together, mystical and sane.
What he has discovered, now, is his isolation.
It is within his heart and soul, true desolation:
The continuity of life is perfect and complete
Connected lives, no doubt, but there's defeat
Of every plan, all lose all in the battle of conceit.
In his significance this man dies in his deceit.

Yet freed from it, there might be a restitution.
Too late to hope, to soon to judge, his constitution
Distrusts the sirens, despises hope, but cannot quite
Give in, instinct still pushes him towards the light.
Perhaps brute force, maybe divine intent,
Drives him slowly forward in his discontent.
Who are those he loves? How do they connect,
If at all, to this compassionate tin man, reflect
Upon his shiny surface and his empty chest?
Do they love him? Anyone who loves him best?
And was it love that he'd deserted, this November
Or the greater love that waited, if he could remember.

For a mistaken love it was that seems to have gone missing
And a love it was that had assumed life was just for kissing.
Loves these may be, well and good, but for a man beyond
Himself, beyond his limits, out of his time, however fond,

There is an intimacy he has yet to find, an intimacy of mind.
Or soul. Not thought, nor theory, nor belief, not any kind
Of explanation, lust, or savage deduction; he needs a fusion,
A mystic marriage of all and one, a multiple conclusion.
With or within himself or with all else or any other being:
It seems that he is being led towards another way of seeing,
A way that contradicts all that he has thought or felt before,
Leaving in him a wilderness of otherness, chaos at his core.

At first aloneness keeps him company, an old and trusted friend
Except its power has multiplied and isolation has no end.
He wakes afraid and lonely, knowing nothing, nowhere to go,
Not at all the old Zen master, serene from top of head to toe:
That was just one more delusion, as if the ending was secure:
Instead an endless wandering, always wondering, never sure.
Still this state of contained being is itself the home of love
If love is redefined, a state of consciousness, a sanctuary above
The atmosphere of knowledge, the clouds of unsure surety,
Where the mind and heart may merge into a bond of purity.
He leaves his clockwork dream, walks out into the alien sun
There is no other way for him, if love is said and fully done.

## Essay 9
## Perfect Disaccord in the
## Quotidian Quiddity Quintet
Starring Rocky, Ellen, Marcus, Ruthie and Cleo
Five characters in search of meaning in
their apparent lives.
### OR
## What and whose reality is it?

Reality Bubbles drifting in the Atmosphere of an Autumnal Afternoon

**Rocky: (Mystic, songwriter, healer, meditator, paradisio)** 'Oooh! Not me first! Hee, hee, hee. Well. All right. What can I say?' (Smiles, charmingly, the gap between his front teeth making him look puckish and mildly louche. He rolls his eyes. first upwards and then side to side. He is obviously thinking.) 'Well. My neighbour has just died. She was very ill. I have been worrying about her for weeks. I wonder what will happen to her, now. She has probably gone to a better place. The place of angels, maybe, though I'm not sure I go along with that. I'm not sure about angels. But I am sure there's something out there. Well, there has to be hasn't there?'

**Ellen: (Retired writer and painter, a healer looking for joy and freedom)** 'Steve's father-in-law has just died, too. He asked to be NFR. He had been brought back too many times and couldn't face it again. He has suffered terribly. (The others ask her to explain.) He had a series of strokes and then a fit. He collapsed in his kitchen and was taken to A & E and when they sent him home again he fell down again and broke his neck. Then he got pneumonia and was also paralysed from the chest down. He was a lovely man, too. He couldn't talk to his family because he had a tube in his mouth and the medics had removed his teeth to make way for the tube. Dying is really the most obscene business for so many of us. Why…?'

**Rocky:** (who has worked in a hospital in the past) 'But why did they remove his teeth? I've never heard of that before (looks shocked and affronted).'

**Marcus: (Cynical, creative-artistic, non-believer in anything whatever.)**

'They were probably dentures.'

**Rocky:** 'I was beginning to wonder if that was the case. God, what an awful story. My neighbour had a very long and painful end. I did all I could to help her. It almost makes you wonder if it's all worth it - but of course it is, it must be. I usually feel that there is something just beyond myself watching and helping . . .'

**Marcus:** 'If there is, it's making a pretty poor job of it - part of the generally lousy creation if there was one, which is highly unlikely. I can't believe the idiocy of people who actually want to come back after death. Once is too often for me.

**Ruthie: (Proto-Buddhist, healer, horse-person, wanderer.)**

'Oh, no. It's not like that at all.'

**Marcus:** 'You think it's all worthwhile, then? But you don't presumably believe that you will return as identifiably the you that is here now? If you come back it could be as anything, couldn't it?'

**Rocky:** 'Is that what you think, Marcus? I thought you were anti-reincarnation.'

**Cleo: (Hierarchical reincarnationist looking to the heavens.)**

(Looking askance at Marcus). 'I agree with Ruthie. It isn't as you say, Marcus. I haven't lived this life and done all this work and put up with everything and tried to develop spiritually, just to return as a dung-beetle. We are here to learn and develop and when we die we go on to something else, to a higher plane if we deserve it. This body is of no importance, it is just the present vehicle of the soul or whatever, which will go on for ever . . . '

**Ellen:** 'That's what I'd like to believe, if only I could. I certainly feel there is something beyond us and I have had enough supernormal experiences to make me suspect that we may continue after death in some way - but how and what? I have no idea. What do you think, Ruthie?'

(Before she can reply, Rocky and Marcus have an interchange on Tibetan theories of the bardo and whether the monsters and angels appearing in the awareness are me how real or mere dream figures. Marcus has encountered them in an 'aura-balancing' ritual with a female shamanic choir but considers the beings in the bardo to be most probably in his own consciousness - Rocky doesn't think this gives them due weight . . . )

**Ruthie:** (when she can get a hearing for her quiet, hesitant, voice) 'It's really rather different from what we have been saying. These images are metaphors or helpful fantasies whereby the soul can migrate to the necessary place, a transmigration, a liberation actually, but it's not perceived as quite the same process as described by Cleo.' (She pulls a sheet of paper from her handbag and asks if she may read it out:

*(The Bardo Thotrol) from Tibetan Buddhism was traditionally read aloud to the dying to help them attain liberation. It guides a person to use the moment of death to recognize the nature of mind and attain liberation. It teaches that awareness once freed from the body, creates its own reality like that of a dream. This dream projection unfolds in predictable ways in ways both frightening and beautiful. Peaceful and wrathful visions appear, and these visions can be overwhelming. Since the awareness is still in shock of no longer being attached to and shielded by a body, it needs guidance and forewarning so that key decisions that lead to enlightenment are made. The Tibetan Book of the Dead teaches how one can attain heavenly realms by recognizing the enlightened realms as opposed to being drawn into the realms of seduction that pull incorporeal awareness into cyclic suffering.*

**Rocky:** 'That sounds pretty sensible. But I'm not sure about the cyclic suffering bit. Does this mean that we have to work at it after we're dead. I can't quite see how we'd do that. Cleo's idea seems more congenial; I mean, that we have to do the work during life to justify a good post-life?'

**Marcus:** 'What shines forth for me, in all this speculation, is that nobody, no-one anywhere, has the faintest clue about any of this. It's absolutely mind-boggling mystery. There really is no such thing as knowledge, just maybe information.

**Ellen:** 'Oh spare me the pessimism. Give us a song, Rocky.'

**Cleo:** 'This is a real problem - I mean, why can't each person have their own truth? We all have to believe in something, don't we? There has to be a reason for being here. A belief is like the body, just something to live inside: the actual soul is absolute and passing through to higher forms . . . '

**Ellen:** 'Even if Marcus is right, and even if his reasoning is perfectly correct, we are still free to **feel** what is important to us. He is being a mind-sadist, making us suffer for his own pleasure'.

**Marcus:** 'I wish! Ellen, my love, you have the cart before the donkey. I am saying that it's the people who set up beliefs – usually to control others - that are the actual sadists… and we are the donkeys!'

(Rocky has been tuning the guitar and now sets off on one of his protest lieder, written by himself and very good, if not entirely understandable in the half - American patois of the lyrics. Then he sings another. There is a devotional atmosphere in the room. Rocky looks around the group lovingly at the end. Marcus congratulates him.)

**Marcus:** 'That was so good. I wonder if I might share with you a poem I have written about my encounter with music?' (They agree and he reads the poem to them.)

## An Die Musik

A flaxen-headed choirboy, I was set to please,
Yearning, archetypal, yet somehow ill at ease,
Sang carols cold on doorsteps, spirit full a thrill,
When that dream died, still uneasy as in its life
And lay unquiet in its grave, regretful shadows rife:
Broken voice, now, broken hopes, no longer winging.
But, hiding my unease, new hope to me came singing

Concertos, symphonies, and string quartets disposed
Love upon me, and they my all too human voice deposed
Now were the years of listening, discovering, and learning
That subdued, or pacified, the voice's everlasting yearning.

Two musics in my ear, one of strings, or brass or wind of wood
The other crooning casanovas, sweet jezebels, bad or good,
Until I walked the winter journeys of a German baritone:
Dietrich Fischer-Dieskau hustling me upon the gramophone

Not yet, not yet, my musical epiphany had to wait
Until I was nearly old, when it was certainly too late
To become an English baritone however hard they'd try
To resurrect the dormant youth and teach him how to fly.

A few years of daily grind took me to the edge of competence,
And singing to an audience was rather more than mere pretence.
For a time I lived that choirboy's dream, tone by joyful tone,
But there was another ringing in my head, a frantic telephone.

I had learned the way to sing, but wasn't it an empty shout?
This performance was just old egotism putting its ugly self about.
Could a singer tell a story without the need for sweet applause?
Wasn't it the moment to reconsider, to take a pregnant pause?
So, at last, I did. It was a dramatic, if not tragic, confrontation.
The shaky treble of the child seemed to echo in my concentration.
This was not the way to end, with Schubert's Will-'o-the Wisp,
I had some life to live before my conversion into a potato crisp.

**Cleo, Ruthie, Ellen, Rocky:** (Spontaneously morphing into a Greek chorus) 'That's so sad. You feel so bad. We feel so bad. Are you raving mad? What's that about ego? A dirgeful farrago. Why suffer so? Sinking so low. It's natural to sing. Not an ego-thing. Spirit takes wing. Ring-a-Ding-Ding We all like to share. Lay our souls bare. Have a care. Great gurus dare. Ring your message out. Sing and shout. Put it all about. Free from doubt. Follow the Dalai Lama. Watch your karma. Keep to your holy dharma.

**Marcus:** 'Yeah. Yeah. Okay. I am not getting through to you. I'm just saying that I want to escape from egotism. It's a painful place once you recognise it. I'd guess that the Dalai Lama has big trouble with it ...'

**Ruthie:** 'I am sure that his Buddhist holiness is without ego altogether'

**Rocky:** 'Dat emperor has chucked away his gear my dear. Ha, ha, ha. Actually, when I've done a gig and people applaud me I do feel good. But I wouldn't call that ego. Isn't it just making a good connection? I mean, it's more like love than egotism, surely?

**Marcus:** 'Let's try another angle: I'm only questioning Unitary Certainty as a philosophy. The cosmic immensity is just too complex and beyond our minds for us to have any idea about it; therefore, we ought to be very, very, very, very much more humble - whether about our so-called achievements or rights to post-mortem continuation in one way or another. In a small shell of the nut, I am saying that we are all pathologically arrogant.'

**Chorus**:

'That is a far too severe assessment of the human race.
You are so hard on yourself if that's your personal case;
Because you're nicer than that, you must know you are,
And there's no need to go to extremes: you go far too far.
In the wrong direction, too; it can't be comforting for you
To see yourself so grimly even if your picture's true.
Your poor soul must suffer agonies of existential grief
So why not cheer yourself with blissful spiritual relief?'

**Rocky**: 'Just relax and let your mind expand into the numinous expanse'

**Ellen:** 'I think your uncertainty is a perfectionist streak of pure hubris'

**Ruthie:** 'That's a bit hard on him he's only trying to be honest (if misled)'

**Cleo:** 'We have to believe in something, Marcus, or life is just a bad joke'

**Marcus:** 'I will say this only once (on this occasion): I come back to the word 'unitary' and the certainty you apply to it. It may be my illusion, but it seems to me that each of you assumes that you are an indivisible, single, entity; that is, a person, a being, that was born, grew up, developed a personality with certain identifiable traits, and that this unity has a cosmic place and relevance, as an individual, and will, should, or may, continue in some form after corporeal death. Is that my illusion or is that what each of you takes as the truth?'

(The chorus takes a break. Coffee, tea, or toilet trips. Marcus sits waiting.)

**Cleo:** 'We have compared notes and agree that you are broadly correct in your assumptions about us. But we also agree that these things are true - basically and really true. So it's just your opinion against ours. And as your opinion is so negative, even nihilistic, or despairing (heads nod vigorously) we will all stay with our opinions - while respecting yours, obviously, because we realise that you have a considerable intelligence - but you can be wrong - and we think you are, much as we love you…'

There is a prolonged silence, in which Marcus's face carries a cast-down expression as he stares at his feet.

**Ellen:** 'Are you sulking?'

**Marcus:** 'Perhaps; but it feels more like an ego skirmish and I don't know the battle - plan. I feel the force of your aggregate opposition and I do understand it. But there's a false focus in here somewhere.

**Rocky:** 'That's serious. That would be real bad, man. What's false, for you?'

**Marcus:** 'OK. Here's a truth. Whatever it might mean: I used to be a biologist, remember? Well here's a biology lesson for you: there are up to 100 trillion (10 to power of say 14) cells in the human body (and ten times as many bacteria, mostly helpful lodgers good for the body's health) so how much sense does it make to see a person as unitary? Especially as all the cells are dying and being replaced every second of existence. A person is a vast and complex ever-changing universe of its own. The interesting question is how does it get to have an awareness of its 'self'? And what is that awareness and what's it 'worth'? Just think, 100,000,000,000,000 tiny, complete, selves as cells, a co-operative of billions comprising each of you and me, with 1,000,000,000,000,000 co-habiting micro-aliens as well. And you think of yourselves as **unities**. You even have a complete seven-yearly cell-replacement. Where's the unitary self in all of this? What is it, if it exists? Each of us is an ocean. As well as all this there are the quantum fields of all these infinitesimally small worlds we are made of, and the electrons talk to each other everywhere. I mean, dearly beloved ones, ain't you being just a tad simplistic?'

### The Chorus silently, privately, contemplates Hidden Questions

**Why do we meet?** It is not just Marcus, the Trouble-Maker. He's actually quite good fun. And he sometimes makes you think. You don't have to agree with him. We all argue anyway, if not as passionately and noisily as he does. There's something else going on. It seems almost as if this is a really safe place. We could be brothers and sisters in spirit. I would miss it if we never met again.

**Is there love?** No doubt at all. It's the spirit-thing. Each of us knows the others care about truth and love and beauty, and that there is freedom about the expression of these spiritual realities; there's no doctrine, no dogma, and no punishment. The level of respect amongst the arguing is overwhelming. Yes there is love.

**Is there any point?** In the sense of 'purpose' or 'outcome', there probably is not any point. Which is probably the point, in another sense. The tone of the meetings is that *being is what matters.* Each of us struggles to find our individual being. Nearly all of life as we live it is concerned with *doing,* and doing leaves no room for being. Even a chapel service somehow focuses on the doing of 'service' or 'worship' or 'celebration', and the singing and declaiming and witnessing are all fine except that they don't necessarily take us into being. On the other hand, meditation or healing, valuable as they are, don't quite cross the boundary and become just being. Crazy argument, paradoxically can achieve it, providing each of us feels perfectly safe.

**Marcus meditatively mulls questionable Hidden Answers**

**There is only love in pure being.**
**There is only beauty in the will to truth.**
**There is only nothing beyond enlightenment.**

*What are these thoughts and where do they come from. Are they just Marcus's fantasies? He is the one who offers them. Are they the next argument? Let them be offered for argument's sake. So long as it is safe. Perfectly safe. In the knowledge that knowledge doesn't really exist and might not matter even if it did . . .*

# Essay 10
# Tao 28

*Lao Tzu seems to have embodied an intuition but had no 'belief-system' and though he is said to have written the Tao-Te Ching, it seems unlikely because he refused to put his thoughts into the written form. He was born about six-hundred years before the start of the Christian Era, and his name is not a real name, but an honorific title (Old Master). I can only assume, as I have with Jesus, half a millennium later, that Lao Tzu is actually an omnibus of wisdom turned into a persona. Taoism seems to be indifferent to codes and rules and the focus is upon natural living, with goodness and respect for conscience and instinct. While insisting upon simplicity, and its importance for freedom and truth, as well as the need to observe and understand nature, Taoism, with its devotion to 'Emptiness' regards the whole universe as somehow shaped by unspecified 'outside forces'. Power is viewed as a product of personal intuition and Taoism would see it used without force and promoting love. Thus the Tao is a Way of Being of endless and mysterious nothingness in which exists everything. Taoism takes the Void to its heart and lives it, so that there is peace amid strife and love amid anger: the Void rules its dominion gently and unobserved.*

*From 'Mystikosmos' Chapter 14 'The Magi'.*

The Quintet was reduced to a trio, Ruthie having gone in search of the Dalai Lama in India and Rocky being laid up with tonsillitis. Cleo had already led a Healing and Meditation group of about ten people, including Ellen and Marcus. She had there described the grey aura around a large willow tree and its generous energy connection to a severely pruned neighbour, thereby setting Ellen and Marcus the future intent of seeing tree-auras and giving them a new insight into Cleo's mysticism. Further to this, a day or so later, the trio of Cleo, Ellen and Marcus met to see what might happen between them. What happened was Cleo's admission that she felt herself to be a 'bumbler' and Marcus's revelation that he talked too much out of a weird anxiety-generosity. Ellen expressed some impatience with these self-obsessions, especially Marcus's excuse for hogging the limelight.

The scene was therefore set for greater spiritual intimacy. Marcus was told that he did talk a lot but it was all right because he usually came up with something interesting, though he should take greater pains to give space to others. Marcus asked Cleo what was next in her life, as he could see no signs of the bumbling she saw in herself and he felt sure she was aiming towards something or somewhere significant.

**Cleo:** 'I try to live according to the "Tao Te Ching" (if that's how you pronounce it). I find the Tao is the best possible way to be. I think it's wonderful. That is my life-aim.'

**Marcus:** 'So you and I have very similar aims: you follow "emptiness" and I try to follow the "void".

**Ellen and Cleo:** 'What are you talking about? What is this "void" you're always on about?'

**Marcus:** (tediously but typically quoting himself) 'The Buddhists took with them the concept of the Void when they entered China from India, but the Taoists already had the concept of Emptiness. They spent several centuries trying to figure out what the two ideas actually meant. So it's not easy. We in the West took the easy route of calling it "God" but that was a cop-out because "God" is even more fuddled an idea than "Nullity". My idea of the Void is the empty but energy-rich creative nothingness from which all creativity happens. I like the Tao because it's a practical way to live spiritually and well, whatever the arcane philosophy.'

**Ellen:** 'You really do talk too much, you know.'

(Marcus goes to find his copy of 'Tao Te Ching'. He is not quite sure they are all talking about the same thing. He returns with his book. Cleo confirms the title. Marcus reads Verse 28 to share it with Cleo and Ella and establish the book's importance to the trio)

Verse 28 (Chad Hansen translation of Tao Te Ching)
*BALANCING OPPOSITES*

*To know it is male*
*And sustain its female aspect*
*Is to act as the social world's ravine.*
*To act as the social world's ravine,*
*Fix on virtuosity, avoid distraction,*
*And return to infancy.*
*To know it is white*
*And sustain its blackness*
*Is to act as the social world's paradigm.*
*To act as the social world's paradigm,*

*Fix on virtuosity, avoid lapses,*
*And return to the absence of ultimates.*
*To know is sublime*
*And sustain its disgrace*
*Is to act as the social world's valley.*
*To act as the social world's valley,*
*Constant virtuosity is sufficient*
*To return to uncarved wood.*
*If wood is split then regard it as an artefact.*
*Sages use it*
*And are regarded as officials and elders.*
*So great systems do not cut.*

**Ellen:** 'I haven't the faintest idea what that is trying to say.'
**Cleo:** 'Neither have I. It makes no sense.'
**Marcus:** 'I thought I understood it but I actually don't, now I read it again.'

(They look at each other in perplexity for a while. Then Cleo suggests that she sends an email with the translation from her book, which she expects to be more comprehensible because her book is the basis of her life-practice and has always been understandable by her.)

**Cleo's email**

*'Here is verse 28 of the Tao as translated by Stephen Mitchell:*

*Know the male, yet keep to the female;*
*receive the world in your arms.*
*If you receive the world,*
*the Tao will never leave you*

*and you will be like a little child.*

*Know the white, yet keep to the black;*
*be a pattern for the world.*
*If you are a pattern for the world,*
*the Tao will be strong inside you*
*and there will be nothing you can't do.*

*Know the personal, yet keep to the impersonal;*
*accept the world as it is.*
*If you accept the world,*
*the Tao will be luminous inside you*
*and you will return to your primal self.*

*The world is formed from the void,*
*like utensils from a block of wood.*
*The Master knows the utensils,*
*yet keeps to the block;*
*thus she can use all things.'*

The trio is now in Cleo's home, with two greyhounds and with two cats here and there. The three humans absorb the fact that Stephen Mitchell is a genius.

**Marcus Googles:**
***Book Description***
*Publication Date:* **August 28, 1992** *Lao-tzu's Tao Te Ching, or Book of the Way, is the classic manual on the art of living, and one of the wonders of the world. In eighty-one brief chapters, the Tao Te Ching looks at the basic predicament of being alive and gives advice that imparts*

*balance and perspective, a serene and generous spirit. This
book is about wisdom in action. It teaches how to work for the
good with the effortless skill that comes from being in accord
with the Tao (the basic principle of the universe) and applies
equally to good government and sexual love; to child rearing,
business, and ecology. Stephen Mitchell's bestselling version
has been widely acclaimed as a gift to contemporary culture.*

**Biography Stephen Mitchell** *is widely known for his
ability to make ancient masterpieces thrillingly new, to step in
where many have tried before and to create versions that are
definitive for our time. His many books include the bestselling
Tao Te Ching, Gilgamesh, The Book of Job, Bhagavad Gita,
and The Selected Poetry of Rainer Maria Rilke. His web site
is www.stephenmitchellbooks.com.*

(**Marcus** Googles Hansen, to be fair, and discovers
umpteen other translations, it seems as if the West has a
profound love-affair with Tao Te Ching, and Marcus asks
why it isn't having more effect - silly question: where is there
evidence of a profound Zen influence in 10 Downing Street or
the White House? Hansen is shown and heard in interview on
Google and it is not a great revelation.)

**Cleo** decides to buy the Mitchell translation for Ellen and
Marcus.

**Marcus** says this is their big chance to move into the Void
of Being.

**Cleo** gets a thank-you poem from Marcus:

### Where's The Time?

Time and mind climbed Stinchcombe Down
To hear a peal of belling laughter;
Time tripped down and sacked the town
And mind fell grieving after.
Is mind inside its time?
Is time out of its mind?
Both undoubtedly sublime
And both entirely blind
As iodine sublimes into the air
Time unsolidifies within my ear
The little town, in mind so fair,
My time knows is not there.
Snows of wood anemones would drift
Where bluebells soon would blow:
Flowers and girls were in my gift.
But time and mind had let them go.
As if they never were, time away,
And mind flies up a space, awry:
The never-was holds greatest sway
It is bright delusion to this loving eye.
Grand physics spies uneasily on time at all
Seeing it is not there upon the edge of reason
No wonder my sweet allusions fail and fall
As timely mind goes to the knife of treason.
I think I see that place, the fields, the flowers,
Remembering, if I can, not knowing if I do:
I feed on sandwiches of mind and scented hours,
Ghostly bread on bread and void between the two

*Until at last a truth rings out with that invasive bell*
*The world I think I knew is ephemeral as fears;*
*It is not time's fault it tripped and broke the spell.*
*In my mind I made a fancy, a daisy-chain of tears.*

And **Cleo** sends a gracious reply:
'Thanks for the poem - you hadn't read it out the other day.
It's heartbreakingly poignant and very beautiful.

'Tell them to bring hankies to the poetry group if you are
reading it to them.'

**Gosh!**
**And Tao to us all.**

## Essay 11
## Protecting the Divine from Religion

This essay is an account of Marcus's rumination on encounters with Rocky, Cleo, and Ellen as well as on certain Humanist influences, including videos of Stephen Fry and (the regrettably late, having died at 62) Christopher Hitchens.

**Atheism and the Two Gods.**

Whatever the appearances to the contrary, Marcus has an affinity for 'God' that had always seriously irritated him. He once tried to deal with it by flirting with Manichaeism. As Wikipedia puts it:

*Manichaeism taught an elaborate cosmology describing the struggle between a good, spiritual world of light, and an evil, material world of darkness. Through an on-going process which takes place in human history, light is gradually removed from the world of matter and returned to the world of light from which it came. Its beliefs, based on local Mesopotamian gnostic and religious movements, contained elements of Christianity, Zoroastrianism and Buddhism. Manichaeism thrived between the third and seventh centuries, and at its height was one of the most widespread religions in the world. Manichaean churches and scriptures existed as far east as China and as far west as the Roman Empire. Manichaeism survived longer in the east, and appears to have finally faded away after the 14th century in southern China, contemporary to the decline in China of the Church of the East. The original, but now lost, six sacred books of Manichaeism were composed in Syriac Aramaic, and translated into other languages to help spread the religion. As they spread to the east, the Manichaean writings passed through Middle Persian, Parthian, Sogdian, Tocharian and ultimately Uyghur and Chinese translations. As they spread to the west, they were translated into Greek, Coptic, and Latin. The spread and success of Manichaeism were seen as a threat to other religions, and it was widely persecuted in Christian, Zoroastrian, Islamic, and Buddhist cultures.*

In simple terms, Marcus had interpreted Manichaeism as a view of the cosmos in which two equally powerful Gods ruled, one evil and one good, and the human role was to support the good one against the bad one. He could see how the original and complex cosmology of Manichaeism was a distillation of older plus contemporary animistic or polytheistic theologies. And it was an obvious precursor of monotheism long before the ancient Jews actually invented it as Jaweh or Jehova. In many ways, however, Manichaeism was intellectually and ethically superior to the monotheist faiths which eventually came to dominate the West and most of the world. In these Semitic religions (Judaism, Christianity and Islam) the evil god is demoted to Satan and the dominant survivor of the pair is somehow supposed to be benevolent (even if occasionally angry, jealous, or vengeful, like any good human father). This untidy resolution meant that millions who worship one of the three possible gods (leaving aside Jesus or the 'holy ghost', who complicate matters even more) are never quite sure whether to blame or be grateful for the mishaps that nature inflicts upon them, yet feel obliged to praise the designated deity however bad things get.

## Marcus the Committed Atheist

He could just cope with the idea of nature not giving a damn for its creatures. It had taken him several decades to come to terms with the bloodiness mixed with loveliness inherent in nature (or the god personifying nature) but he had never adjusted to the peculiar habit of those who persisted in seeing god/nature as bountifully, generously, well-disposed towards any animal, including or particularly the human variety. His passionate anger was driven, apparently, by what he regarded as the lies and evasions involved in seeing 'God' as human-loving, the personal, father-god perpetrated by religions. His rage had seemed excessive to others and was even an embarrassment to himself. Why should he care, he would tell himself, if people wanted to behave like childish idiots? It was not a happy state of being for someone who especially and increasingly wanted to dwell in a serene state of aware being. Two other committed atheists seemed to him to dominate the Western zeitgeist: Richard Dawkins and the aforementioned Christopher Hitchens, and they had put over their views in widely selling books, eg, *The God Delusion* and *God is not Great*. Neither of these two men seemed to Marcus to be quite as enraged as himself, though Hitchens came close in a debate on the alleged great benefits of Roman Catholicism over the last two millennia. It was still a problem for Marcus, being close to friends, notably some Unitarians, who did not get so inflamed as he, and who even managed to sing hymns to 'God' regardless of all the evidence of 'His' malignity. Marcus's subconscious came to his rescue (after decades of prodding him from various obscure positions) by dreams that showed him his true motives. Once he saw it, the solution was absurdly obvious.

### Lessons from Nature

From childhood, Marcus had been dazzled by natural beauty. Then, in early puberty, he had been assailed by the bad side of nature. By his thirties, he had become overwrought by the pain, cruelty and waste in the natural world (including and especially the human part of the natural world). Religion outraged him, as mentioned, because it put one or another god in charge and adored and thanked the celestial lord for his good works. This paradoxical or hypocritical view of a supreme architect struck Marcus as insulting lunacy - insulting, that is, to all the life-forms who had to put up with the pain and slaughter ordained by these bloodthirsty godheads. Like Hitchens, Marcus also loathed the behaviour of religions in terms of the pain and slaughter and suppression they imposed on millions of human beings and the other animals. But this, foul as it was, did not constitute Marcus's true motive for his rage. The credibility-gap between his fury and his rational assessment of the evil had become unbearable. He felt a fool, bothering so extremely about the ineluctable horror of the religious theories, beliefs and practices. But how could he stop?

### Spinoza the Deliverer

It had been only a year or two since Marcus had discovered Baruch Spinoza, in a search of true originators of spiritual rationality (Marcus being a mystical rationalist according to his own assessment). In sum, this is the Spinoza that threw Marcus a lifeline (courtesy of Wickipedia): *Spinoza contends that "Deus sive Natura" ("God or Nature") is a being of infinitely many attributes, of which thought and extension are two. His account of the nature of reality, then, seems to treat the physical and mental worlds as one and the same. The universal substance consists of both body and mind, there being no difference between these aspects. This formulation is a historically significant solution to the mind-body problem known as neutral monism. Spinoza's system also envisages a God that does not rule over the universe by providence, but a God which itself is the deterministic system of which everything in nature is a part. Thus, according to this understanding of Spinoza's system, God would be the natural world and have no personality.* The radical idea that 'God' and 'Nature' were the same thing was balm to Marcus's pain, but it still didn't apply morphine to the deepest agony, his Fisher King wound, the fact that the whole human culture tended towards God-obsession rather than take the existential and courageous step of being fully responsible for itself and rebutting delusional beliefs about its supernatural specialness.

**The Divine Void**

Marcus was a Void-lover, the ultimate in Existentialism in that he saw the Void as the ultimate source of all creativity but having no evident substance of its own. The paradox of the absolutely full absolute emptiness had long held firm in the eastern esoteric philosophies and is hard for the occidental mind to grasp. This was the main reason why Marcus had gone on fulminating long after he could have stopped. The problem had been his inherited culture wherein 'clerisy' was implicitly an amalgam of religion and intellect. He had not seen the obvious, i.e. that religion had little or nothing to do with mysticism or divinity. Indeed, most clerics were more likely to torch a mystic or a direct perceiver of the divine than embrace what was a truly and naturally enlightened being.

### Religion was the Enemy of the Divine

(At last the penny dropped with a resounding clang:)

It was perhaps, unintentional, sometimes. But Marcus now realised that religious authority generally strangled innate divinity. His friends, Rocky and Cleo were intimately in touch with the divine and did regard it as absolutely sacred. Their flights of fancy were not part of this divinity, but rather, he perceived, an all-too-human attempt to secure something comforting in a harsh or indifferent world. Ellen had already reached this conclusion by her innate common sense. Which was why she found his fury so irritating.

### Manichaeism Exhumed

In a way, the old duality made a new sense. There was a cosmic battle between the bad and the good. But it was difficult to be sure where the battle lines were drawn. Indeed, it was usually impossible. Marcus had to settle for a state of intelligent ignorance and be content with an untrustworthy world. He decided that he had henceforth to focus his anger on the right target, the clerics, or keep it under lock and key.

## Divinity Defined

Marcus was left with the joy of unalloyed acceptance of his basic sense of the divine with freedom from the miasma of religion. But he still needed a fully realised form of the divine that did not involve fanciful belief systems. In other words, he needed a form for his mystical rationality, an apparent paradox. The Void was his prototype, as it were. It had sustained him as an idea for several years. But he needed to have a more accessible metaphor. The Void, for all its cosmic value to him, still suffered, as a word, with the sense of emptiness. That was something he had repeatedly needed to explain and investigate. Thanks to Cleo, Marcus now received a form of words that fulfilled the need to define the Divine. It was still the Void, yet it was also a fulsome concept for existence as a human being.

## The Tao

Having belatedly understood what the Tao offered him, Marcus saw that his life would be refashioned according to it. This was essentially the process of walking that path. Two verses from Stephen Mitchell's translation of the Tao Te Ching made the point:

### *Verse Five*

*The Tao doesn't take sides;*
*it gives birth to both good and evil.*
*The Master doesn't take sides;*
*she welcomes both saints and sinners.*

*The Tao is like a bellows:*
*it is empty yet infinitely capable.*
*The more you use it, the more it produces;*
*the more you talk of it, the less you understand.*

*Hold on to the centre.*

### Verse Six
*The Tao is called the Great Mother:*
*empty yet inexhaustible,*
*it gives birth to infinite worlds*
*It is always present within you.*
*You can use it any way you want*

# Essay 12
# Tao or Ockham

*And the tall, weak, strong man, haunted by abandonment,*
*But resolute and accepting of all things, stands his shifting ground:*
*He is determined to survive, in some degree or form, surrendered.*
*(from Essay Seven, end of 'The First Man' poem)*

*Hope and fear are both phantoms*
*that arise from thinking of the self.*
*When we don't see the self as self,*
*what do we have to fear?*
*(from Tao Te Ching, verse 13, Stephen Mitchell translation)*

The 'tall, weak, strong man' died a few weeks after the poem was written. We may as well call him Adam. He was a cultured, musical, Christian who practised complementary medicine. He was no Ockham. As do many intelligent English persons, he preferred to elaborate possibilities, including the extraordinary idea of literal resurrection. Apart from Marcus, who, like Ockham, refused to 'multiply entities beyond necessity', the members of the Quotidian Quiddity Quintet (Q3 for short) favoured various forms of 'complementary' reality. Marcus, too, liked to imagine different realities, but he would not concrete them into beliefs, or even firm hopes, as did the other four. Adam was never a Q3 associate, except that he often met Ellen and Marcus, together with his wife, as a spiritually enquiring group of four. The possible interactions between Adam and Rocky, Cleo and Ruthie, plus Ellen and Marcus, are the basis of this essay, although it is impossible to say how that particular reality might have actually appeared. So this is a fairy story.

### Elaboration of The Six

*(As we are in the world of 'elaboration of entities', here is a **Numerological** portrait of a **Six Person**, showing the eclectic, even random, distribution of qualities in such elaboration concept... Ockham would be turning in his superfluous grave: **Good**: intellectual creativity, discrimination, imagination, love, perfection, relatedness, conventionality, healing and nurturing idealism, empathy, sympathy, unconditional love, grace, simplicity, reliability. **Bad**: aloofness, complexity, weakness, impracticality, submissiveness, shallowness, restlessness, selfishness, weak - willedness. Incidentally but not unimportantly, the 'Six' is also one of the nine basic personality types of the ancient and modernised **Enneagram,** a type that is ruled by fear and follows the leader slavishly, and otherwise called The Questioner or The Trooper. These are, evidently enough, separate, different, and unconnected classification systems. Beware systems!)*

**A room in an old coach-house. It is in a quiet side-street, which is an appropriate site for a meeting place of Unitarian Universalists. Plus a Christian on this occasion. Present: Adam, Cleo, Ellen, Marcus, Rocky and Ruthie.**

**Rocky:** (after strumming his guitar and lighting the candle) 'I'm glad you're here, Adam, because I wanted to ask you something. Let me first read to you a piece from the internet, it's titled 'Atheism and Agnosticism: Theological Diversity in Unitarian Universalism'. It says: '*Atheists are people who do not believe in a god, while Agnostics are people who think that we cannot know whether a god exists. Both groups are welcome in Unitarian Universalism. Today, a significant proportion of Unitarian Universalists do not believe in any type of god. Our congregations are theologically diverse places where people with many different understandings of the sacred can be in religious community together.*'

So, Adam, while Unitarianism has roots in Christianity, it is now perfectly in order for Unitarians to have no god-belief at all and that includes disbelief in Jesus of Nazareth as divine. If we four, sitting here, were in that category, as we might well be, what would you, as a Christian, think, or say to us?'

**Ruthie:** (while Adam scrutinises the ceiling and rubs his chin) 'That's not fair, Rocky. Adam has no need to explain himself to us. We are all, mercifully, free to think as we like and without criticism from anyone else. We met today to celebrate existence not argue about gods.'

**Rocky**: 'I know. And I agree. I didn't want an argument about gods. I just wanted to hear Adam's thoughts. Why shouldn't we be curious about each other? In fact, if we're not, what's the point of meeting. Should we just sit here and say nothing at all.'

**Adam:** 'Thanks Ruthie, but I rather agree with Rocky. It's just rather difficult to say anything about my faith to people who don't share it. Yet we ought to be able to communicate, however diversely.'

**Cleo:** 'It's not about "ought", surely. Don't you mean "need", Adam? Or maybe you don't, if your connection with your god is completely sacrosanct?'

**Marcus:** 'Come on Adam: you and I have been around this carousel a few times and I know you like to reveal your truth to receptive ears. Well, these people may be unbelievers, but they are far from closed-minded. Unless you are a stickler for the party-line, which I think you're not, you'll get a better hearing from this bunch than from your average Anglican front row. So unless you've got a problem with argument, say your piece and let us say ours.'

**Adam:** 'OK, but I'm going to dodge the god-question, at least for now. I just don't want to get into that minefield. But I will, if you want, discuss with you the issue of salvation or soteriology as it is known in scholarly discourse. I am fairly close to death, personally, so that soteriological matters actually concern me more than ideas about what or whom 'god' may be. Being practical, where am I going and how will it feel to be there? Yes, I know, it is a mystery. But it's bloody interesting to a corpse-to-be. As a topic of light conversation, as it were.'

**Cleo:** 'I don't see how you can separate the two things. Doesn't salvation hinge on the nature of the divine? It's a real, practical question, surely - the biggest question of all and double-barrelled? I mean, if god is an illusion, then salvation is meaningless, isn't it? What would one be saved for or by?'

**Rocky:** 'I'm sorry to quibble, but we are in a sort of slavery here, caught up in life and death, so we do crave for release in some way. I prefer the word 'redemption', the freeing from slavery, to 'salvation', the freeing of humankind from sin, because I don't really buy into the idea of sin unless it is accepted that the universe is full of it - at least that the world is - and that if there were a god then the sin would be his sin, the idea of Jesus being the son of god come to earth to save us from our sins is ludicrous as the author of the sins is god himself (and Jesus too, if he's a god) . . . .

**Ellen:** 'Some quibble! But he has a point, Adam, doesn't he? I mean, why do you assume that you need to be forgiven by some god for the way you've lived your life? It must be that you are looking for post-mortem favours of some kind. To the Christian, life seems to be a protection-racket with god as the head of the celestial Mafia. Is that how you see it, Adam? Are you looking for a safe passage to heavenly peace?'

**Adam:** 'I'm not sure there's any point in my being here. You are all so unforgiving, even spiteful. Well, perhaps this is my test. Maybe God has set me this travail to test me. I will try to rise above the mud, like a lotus flower. Are you all prepared to listen to me? (There is general assent except from Ruthie, who reserves her position, saying that she has a completely different idea, for sharing later.) You have to accept that I am a Christian and that it's a matter of faith. You have expressed views that are repellent to me and I don't have to dispute with you. I won't dispute with you, in fact, because that would demean my faith. All I can do is tell you how I experience the divine in the closing part of my earthly existence. That should be more than enough for you and for my God.

**Marcus:** 'No dispute necessary, or even desirable. For me, this is a learning experience, a situation in which we as human beings can try to address serious matters of how to live and die. We can't teach each other, but we can learn from each other. Adam's faith is no barrier to dialogue so long as he does not find our different faith a barrier to dialogue. So interchange can be achieved, surely? Particularly important is Adam's approaching demise: can we help him make it as good as he wants it to be?'

(There's general and emphatic agreement, particularly to the last sentence.)

**Adam:** 'Thank you. It isn't easy. Maybe I should begin by saying that I am really frightened, and not sure what is frightening me. I feel bad about this. I should feel safe in God's hands. But I don't think I do. I'm not sure. I ask myself if this is a failure of my faith, it sounds dreadful, but am I lacking in trust as well as faith, I wonder. It is true that I need salvation and probably redemption as well. Apart from weakness of faith in the Almighty, have I done enough to cleanse myself and my soul for entry into the Kingdom of Heaven. And what will happen to me if I haven't? I am in eternal danger. At least, my soul may be. I ought to be looking forward in joy to the next stage of my journey, not shaking with terror. I thought that pain would be my main problem but it is actually fear. This is the very thing that Christians defeat by their faith and here am I failing in the basic process. Can you atheists help? Surely not!'

**Ruthie:** 'I can offer something that might give a different angle to the problem - after all, we all suffer from it in one way or another. I suggest that the pitfall for the Christian is in the focus on self. Remember that you have 'inherited' a god with a strong ego and that you as a human also have a strong ego. It is actually the Western mindset. We are all about ego, and our concept of higher being is not entirely free from the urge to achieve in some way. In my opinion, and in my heart, it seems absurd to have to worry about your level of achievement at the same time as being frightened of dying and death. This is an appalling burden put on humankind by the Abrahamic religions. Absolutely poisonous. The thing is, it's not necessary. I know you have this faith of yours, Adam, but it is not as absolute as you have been encouraged to believe. There are other concepts, equally or even better adjusted to human needs and aspirations - as well as being kinder to the other forms of life.'

**Adam:** 'I find this really threatening but I have also to admit there is a sort of hope in it as well. You are saying that this isn't my only option? If so, are you trying to suggest that atheism would let me off some sort of hook? That would be craven, disloyal and criminal of me. It would be the opposite of salvation. I would be steeped in sin. Yet I confess to a flicker of interest, God help me!'

**Ruthie:** 'I said that the problem was the focus on self. Can I say a bit more about that, Adam? It might be relevant. It won't hurt you to listen. At least, it might, if I tell you that you are too much into your personal pride. You are too self-important, Adam. All Christians are. All the Abrahamics foster colossal self-importance - while preaching submission and humility before one of their deities. It's a perfect non-win scenario for a mere human.

**Adam:** 'So you are adding the agony of self-abnegation to my pile of horrors. Thanks!

**Ruthie:** 'Well, why not? But you should be careful with this: self-abnegation is putting oneself aside in favour of others. That could be seen as very Christian. I didn't mean that. I meant putting the self aside *completely.* A large proportion of your suffering would be discarded in the process.'

**Adam:** 'I see where that is leading. Straight to Buddhism, obviously. But I am not a Buddhist. And I don't see how soul fits into that equation - it's all a question of soul isn't? Even for an atheist? Or don't you think soul exists either? I'm sorry, but none of this is helping me at all.'

**Ellen:** 'Oh damn these words. Damn the ideologies too. Does it really matter a fig what any of us believe? Especially as we know nothing. Are we so dumb that we can't find any comfort for Adam, or for any one of us for that matter?'

**Cleo:** 'I agree with that. But Ruthie was saying something valuable, I think. I have to use damned words for this, so please try to read between the lines. There is a trap in the idea of self and it contaminates the idea of soul as well. It's this state of personal possession that gives us so much trouble. We really do seem to be incapable of the freedom that comes with moving aside from self. Look, Adam, what is it, actually, that scares you? Pain? Loss? Non-existence? Post-mortem punishment? What?' (She gets up from her seat and goes to Adam, putting her hand on his arm. Adam weeps like a child.

Cleo holds him in her arms. There is a long pause while the room becomes charged with emotional energy. Then Cleo sits down on the floor in front of Adam, holding his hand.)

**Cleo:** 'I have a problem not unlike yours, Adam. I have a health-condition that causes some concern. And I want to have an after-life. I have made a belief-system for myself that keeps me happy. I persuade myself it is really true. But is it? Really? Who knows? Then, on the other hand, I am a follower of the Tao, which I do trust completely, but which offers nothing concrete. Just a beautiful emptiness. I have no place in that as an individual, as an ego, nor probably even as a soul. It would be best for me to shift from the spiritual evolution idea that I have made into a faith and go into the open being of Tao if I could. I suspect that Ruthie might have been saying something like that.' (Cleo looks round at Ruthie inviting her response.)

**Ruthie:** 'It's true that I am inclined to Buddhism and I like the idea of non-selfness together with relieving suffering. But the Tao sounds wonderful. I must learn more about it. The trouble is, how could an ancient Chinese philosophy help a person like Adam, who is utterly absorbed by self-based monotheism. It's too big a leap, surely?'

**Ella:** 'Well, that's interesting. Adam actually practises ancient Chinese medicine. He is deeply convinced by it. I have always wondered how he integrated ancient Chinese medicine and ancient Jewish religion. It mightn't be too difficult, Adam, for you to introduce the Tao into your life; you're halfway there already, aren't you?' (Adam explodes with a sort of laugh that is also a snort of disgust. He obviously considers the women to be talking nonsense. His face registers contempt for their simple-mindedness. He looks like an angry arch bishop.)

**Marcus:** 'What is the answer, Adam? Don't just close your mind on it. Why not the Tao? You might be able to put down all the Abrahamics, as Ruthie calls them, and find a completely new serenity in the brilliance of Lao Tze, as he is called. Ah, I perceive a new problem. You don't know anything about the Tao, do you? It's been there all your life, next to the ancient medicine, and you've ignored it. How crazy is that?'

**Adam:** 'Of course I know about the Tao. And Buddhism. They're just not for me. You have no conception of the vast importance of Jesus Christ, have you? The miracle of Jesus transcends all other human experience and thought. That is my reality. It is an absolute.'

**Marcus:** 'It is beyond permissable discussion, then? You are so certain of it that we could say nothing of importance about it?'

(Adam remains silent for several long minutes. The others sit and wait for him to speak. The atmosphere in the room becomes increasingly heavily charged.)

**Adam:** 'I think you cannot possibly understand the sheer immensity of the Christian view of existence.'

**Ellen:** 'Why not? Are we too stupid?'

**Adam:** 'No, of course not. You just haven't been called, I guess. That's not your fault though it may be your misfortune.'

**Cleo**: 'What is "called"? Has the divine given you specific instructions? I don't mean that sarcastically. I'm serious. Do you feel that Jesus Christ has "called" you?'

**Adam:** 'That's personal. You can't expect me to tell you that.'

**Ellen:** 'Again, why not? You have asked us to help you. We need to know why you are so determined to remain a Christian even though it's not making you happy.'

(Adam becomes angry and speaks very loudly.)

**Adam:** 'I should have bloody well known it was daft to talk to you lot. You have no idea of the sacred. You just go into your sodding heads and do amateur theology. Leave it to the experts. You're just so out of your depth . . .'

(Ellen also in a loud voice and interrupting. Then quietening down after the first two sentences. She becomes affectionate and warm.)

**Ellen:** 'We are not. You are very transparent, Adam. You wear Christianity as a badge and are unable to practise it, otherwise you wouldn't be so damned scared. You're just plain scared of death, as we all are, and you have displaced it onto the jury up in heaven that almost certainly is just a figment of human delusion. Also, while we are on the subject, let me tell you that you, like the rest of the Abrahamicals, are confusing Christian faith and morality. You said at the beginning that you were afraid of being judged negatively. As if Christians had a prerogative on good behaviour. That's the age-old story and it's a lie, Adam. We atheists are just as concerned about morality as you are, only more so probably. So tell me what is really bugging you, as I don't accept the divine judgement story. Why are you afraid, really?'

**Rocky:** 'I know what's scaring him. I can feel it too. I think he is afraid that the whole pack of cards is falling down around him. I mean, the assumed importance of humankind is on the line here. What if we are wrong in our assumption that we are the whole point of life on earth? What if god/nature doesn't give a monkey's for the specialness of any species including us? The evidence, such as it is, points in that direction. Adam is basically aware that he is nothing special, never was anything special, and never will be anything special. If you have been trying to believe the opposite all your life but failed to be really convinced that it really is bloody terrifying . . . .(Adam has passed out and fallen to the floor. The others crowd around him. They try to revive him. But they discover that he is dead. It must be a heart-attack, they assume. This is eventually confirmed by paramedics. The corpse is taken away and the five remaining characters sit for a long time and look at one another.)

**Rocky:** (Eventually) 'Well, we solved his problem for him. Didn't we?'

**Ellen:** 'Oh don't be such a bastard, Rocky. You look as if you're bloody glad he's gone. A man has died here, now, as a result of being with us, and you talk as if he's been booked into a taxi and on the way home.'

**Cleo:** 'That's actually true, in a way. Adam was a bit like me. I want to follow the Tao but I can't resist the blandishments of reincarnation. That's a split in my psyche. Like his split between ancient Chinese medicine and ancient Abrahamicalism . . .'

**Ruthie:** 'I don't see that as the split. The problem is that we know instinctively that we live in the Void, the creative but neutral space, yet we want the universe to love us. One partnership worse than a "rock and a hard place" is a "struggle and a fantasy". Who wants to struggle, really?'

# Essay 13
# Circle of Seven

**The Circle 1 Eliza:** old, physically strong, intelligent, lonely and angry. **2 Carrie:** young, vigorous, imaginative, visionary, burdened. **3 Marcus:** old, damaged, vigorous, intellectual, mystical, creative. **4 Eve:** recently widowed, determinedly positive, caring, assertive. **5 Catherine:** young, spontaneous, mildly bipolar, addictive personality. **6 Stefan:** oldish, damaged, unstable, searching, intuitive, caring. **7 Ellen:** old, damaged, wise, lapsed-creative, anxious, intuitive-intelligent.

**The Stories** (as told on this occasion)

**Eliza.** A vague, scatty, aura pervades, nowadays, but her determination to live and to live well carries her along. In this circle she focuses entirely on the problems of lost powers (of memory, especially) and the misery of having to depend on others. This translates into irritation at being told what is good for her and being treated as less able and commanding than she actually is. The principal target of her wrath on this occasion is her long-serving home-help, who is also apparently strong-minded and strong-willed. (Eliza is also known to be furious about her stepson's approach to her finances, helping her in ways she finds patronising and unimaginative). It is hard to resist the feeling that she protests too much, as if her declining mental powers were somehow involved in her spleen, which is at variance with her inherent capacity for affection and kindness. The group takes her seriously and tries to help. On the assumption that the home-help is pre-empting Eliza's ideas about her home-life, the group suggests that Eliza might gain leverage by pre-empting the pre-emptor. Could Eliza create A List Of Important Things and present it to the home-help as soon as she arrives? This would be The List of Vital Tasks. The fascistic cleaner would just have to get on and do them. Eliza is startled by the obvious power waiting in her hands. She says she will do it. There is, however, no obvious zeal for the change of management style in her household. Eliza seems to have reached a stage in her life where she feels hog-tied by horrible reality. It might almost seem that she prefers inner anger to actual confrontation. In a sense, it is a safe strategy: there is the satisfaction of an imaginary onslaught upon the opponent without the risk of retaliation. The unavoidable or accidental or deliberate self-weakening implicit in this process could be a concomitant of the ageing process. After all, this society does now categorise old people as essentially superfluous, unlike previous times when age was venerated and wisdom assumed to be forthcoming from ancient lips. Eliza would be a powerful soothsayer in such a culture. She is intelligent and highly educated and has suffered a long and eventful life. How could she not be an inspiration to the less mature ranks of society? Hence her anger towards her well-intentioned helper may actually be a displaced passion, one more properly warranted by a perceived hubris of elected dictators and self-styled know-alls that abound upon our television screens and in universities and council offices. Eliza could be seen as the casualty of a youth-based, throw-away, consumer-driven, cult of triviality. It is a terrible irony that a person who tries to cope with the traumata of ageing is so weakened and infantilised, while actual children are treated as little gods. Is it all about the suppressed terror of death?

**Carrie.** Almost, but not quite, the other side of the coin, Carrie's shining sweetness and robust common sense are under great pressure from a mother who no longer has any real relationship with Carrie but somehow achieves the enslavement of her daughter in the daily grind of keeping the old woman alive. It is, perhaps, the ultimate 'hiding to nothing', a lose/lose situation. There is, as usual, a sister who keeps clear of trouble, leaving it all to Carrie - or so it seems. The mother has virtually ceased to function as a distinct and self-responsible adult. Just as our society wastes the virtues of age, it also perpetuates the horror of pathological uselessness. So Carrie tells her sad story and the group listens attentively, just as they did to Eliza. If the connection between the two stories occurs to anyone in the group, no-one dares to point it out. Carrie has somehow got to rid herself of the burden of her mother. Eliza is becoming a burden and fighting to hold on to her autonomy. The answer in both cases is that the aged person has to be 'managed' in a civilised, compassionate and creative manner. Sooner or later, Eliza will slip into the grey zone where she is primarily a vacant presence. She is not free to escape that by medical means as clerics rule that particular roost. Religion condemns her to a living death, and she knows it. Carrie's mother seems not to be that lucid, which in a way is easier because she can be parked in a temporary half-mortuary euphemistically called an old people's home. Here, again, clerisy rules and wasteful maintenance achieves absolutely nothing. The answer to the problem is not very hard to deduce. Just as children have to be managed for life, old people should be managed for death. It should be approached with interest and even delight, like a long and well-deserved night's sleep. The group doesn't discuss this. There's no appetite for it. But only because it is banned by the dictatorship, the diabolical coalition of church and state. Everywhere, generally, more and more people are accepting, indeed longing for, the relief of assisted and painless suicide. It is a growing need, but it is being stifled. The group only talks, therefore, of the miserable palliative of geriatric nursing or its more realistic twin, hospice care. This is the path that Carrie must make her mother follow. It is a path inherently abhorrent to Carrie, for whom life and death are a continuum of adventure and fascination. But her own life is being laid waste by her mother's wretchedness. The door is marked: No Way Out and the group and Carrie tire of the pointless prodding of the half-corpse. Sensing the general feeling, Carrie smiles happily and talks about her dogs. They are, appropriately, a mother and pup. No problems there, except the cutting grief of having to part some day with a stricken friend where the clerics do not interfere. She paints a vivid and beautiful word-picture of the two dachshunds lying fast asleep on their backs, paws in the air, in Carrie's sitting room; a human being and two beloved canines in comfort and safety. The group comes alive and awake with laughter and loving imagination. They all know what actually matters. There is this sublime pleasure of connectedness, whether between people or dogs or cats, or budgerigars, and this continuum is beyond price and only sullied by human greed or power-lust. The group of seven people becomes a haven, in which sacred imagination flourishes. Thanks to dachshunds and Carrie's lovely good sense.

**Marcus.** Is in a playful mood which, for him, means that he wants to trek through some part of his internal jungle. He tends easily to let people see into him, though he doesn't always like the result of their scrutiny: another 'hiding to nothing' perhaps. Marcus is not a betting man, anyway, and doesn't calculate the odds. He just lays down the money wherever he feels an attraction and sees where it goes. He does calculate in another sense, though: he always asks whether an idea is anything but nonsense. Occam's razor matters to him. The stories from Eliza and Carrie have affected him but not made him morose. Instead, he contemplates Stefan's idea of the Inner Child and remembers the contentious discussion reported in Essay One. Since that time, Stefan has found increasing interest in what he calls the 'Divine Child', which seems to carry the symbolism of the 'gold' of childhood and may represent a shift in Stefan's complex psychology. The Divine Child seems important to Marcus and he later discovers the following account:

***According to Candess M. Campbell, PhD, Spiritual Healer (comments excerpted from Caroline Myss):***

*'The Divine Child archetype is closely related to both the*

*Innocent and Magical Child, but is distinguished from them by its redemptive mission. It is associated with innocence, purity, and redemption, god-like qualities that suggest that the Child enjoys a special union with the Divine itself. Few people are inclined to choose the Divine Child as their dominant Child archetype, however, because they have difficulty acknowledging that they could live continually in divine innocence. And yet, divinity is also a reference point of your inner spirit that you can turn to when you are in a conscious process of choice. You may also assume that anything divine cannot have a shadow aspect, but that's not realistic. The shadow of this archetype manifests as an inability to defend itself against negative forces. Even the mythic gods and most spiritual masters - including Jesus, who is the template of the Divine Child for the Christian tradition - simultaneously expressed anger and divine strength when confronting those who claimed to represent heaven while manifesting injustice, arrogance, or other negative qualities. Assess your involvement with this archetype by asking whether you see life through the eyes of a benevolent, trusting God/Goddess, or whether you tend to respond initially with fear of being hurt or with a desire to hurt others first.'*

Whether or not it is the Divine Child archetype that is active in Marcus, there is certainly a tendency in him to experience retrospectively a mystical childhood. In the group he describes the increasing occurrence of his 'snapshots'. He is attracted to them and mystified by them. He asks the group to consider them. Typically, what happens is that Marcus will be doing something like a crossword or a sudoku (significantly, perhaps, play-activities) and there will flash across his awareness an image from his boyhood. These images are fairly constant in that there are only about twenty of them that occur frequently and they only invade his consciousness for a fraction of a second when he is thinking of something quite different. Typical examples are offered to the group:

1. There is a bank on which grow tall conifers and a smaller tree from which he once fell, giving himself a greenstick fracture of his forearm. There is a small walled section of the bank with a hole from which pours constantly clear sparkling water into a large stone trough. This horse trough actually exists in the village of his childhood.

2. A small river passes below a narrow road. At this point Marcus used to play and once fell into the river in his Sunday-best clothes - with dire results when he went home wet and muddy. This spot is not at all negatively affected by the event, quite the reverse.

3. Further up this river there is a private estate which could be entered by jumping the river. Marcus loved this river, at this point and others, and frequently fell or jumped into it.

4. A broad, flat hill, on which a wide variety of wild orchids could be found by Marcus as an aspiring botanist. The strongest image of the hill, among several, is where he first encountered a profusion of early purple orchids.

5. A steep lane up to this hill passes a field just below woods. In the field he once met other youngsters and played in the thick snow. He remembers a strong sexual impulse at

that time.

6. He is working in a small bottling factory and walks out onto a platform from which he can see the woods on the same hill. Mist is clearing in the morning sun. He is overwhelmed by the desire to be on the hill. But he is trapped by the bottling work.

No-one in the group can share these experiences, nor can they respond in any way. Except Stefan, for whom the story confirms his own (different) acquaintance with the divine child archetype. Marcus fails to get any inkling of why the images pop into his mind apparently irrelevantly. Then someone asks how these pictures connect with Marcus's painting. This is a revelation to him. He sees a connection of great importance. To a degree, his painting embodies or manifests his experience of the divine child archetype, though he had not previously realised it. It is as if the images are nudging him to remember where his inspiration actually comes from.

**Eve.** She seems to have retreated, or transcended, into a hermetic state of some kind. She is outwardly the same woman, though perhaps a little tougher, or more brittle, as could be expected of her new situation of widowhood. She used to weep easily in groups, and usually about herself and her psychological and emotional traps. Not now; she is resolutely bright, smiling and composed. Indeed, she asserts that she wishes to maintain a behaviour that she calls her 'bright eyes'. She has already indicated that she won't talk (yet?) about her grief. Rather than sadness or regret or simply loss, she seems to prefer to focus on helping others. She is an Enneagram Two, a Giver, so this is consistent, though not necessarily a good position for her to be in. In this particular group meeting she is almost hidden, in the hermetic sense, and there is no possibility of getting near her emotionally nor psychologically intimate. She says very little and what she does say is conventionally loving and supportive. It would be hard for anyone who doesn't know of her experiences during the last year to realise that she has been through an emotional hell. It is baffling for Ellen and Marcus, who have been her close friends for twenty years, during which time there has been deep interchange on the paths of personal awareness and development. It is not impossible that Eve is in hysterical denial. Her belief-systems, influenced by her attachment to the doctrines of Rudolf Steiner, have always seemed to be oriented to concepts of divinity, yet now she takes a distanced stance, saying that existence, or nature, are neither good nor bad, but that everything merely is as it is. No loving deity, then? Being obliged to have close contact with a lover dying distressfully would require an extreme credo for happiness to prevail. During those months she did seem to have just such a credo. It was impossible to guess whether she realised that the death of her husband, Adam, within a few weeks was the most likely outcome of his illness. It is still not clear how realistic she was. Ellen and Marcus had invited her to work with them on grief, as something affecting all three of them, in different ways but to extensive degree. She had declined, for the time being. This space can only be watched, therefore, and we must wait to see what happens.

**In her own words**: these are Eve's later comments to Marcus on the group meeting:

*"I enjoyed the gathering and the love everybody seemed to be willing to give to the other and the whole group and why are we struggling to give it to ourselves in equal ways. Patsy Rosenberg, author of the book 'The Right to Speak' was on 'desert island discs' on Sunday. It was great to hear her in person. For me she talked a little about the pain of learning to be more fully ourselves - or the pain we are allowed to shed in order to get through to the fuller picture. Which is, I think, what we were on about in the afternoon - how much can we bear to live within our being, you write and in what ways can we lighten our burden?"*

**Catherine.** She was described at the beginning as 'young', but is probably approaching fifty, yet she has the bearing and speech-character of a modern young woman even to the extent of being rather bored with most things except those immediately affecting her. It is a worldly pose, perhaps, because she is actively engaged in healing work of various kinds. She has a changeable nature and is refreshingly direct. For example, Marcus is suffering from redness and swelling of his facial skin which he attributes to psoriasis. It is painful and unsightly. He is unprepared for Catherine's directness in talking about it. She may have experience of it personally as she seems particularly interested and says how unfortunate it is to have it on one's face. (Incidentally the condition is later diagnosed as Rosacea and an antibiotic gel substantially reduces it but that is too late for the group meeting!). At the previous meeting, Catherine was depressed and angry. Much of the energy of that meeting had been consumed by the process of collective empathy. Her relations with men had been mixed, to say the least. Her great love had died young and left an unfillable gap in her life. Then she had an apparently misceginational partnership with a man who seems to have abandoned her and failed to pay his share of the upkeep of their son. In this meeting, she has regained both her poise and her cheerfulness. She refers to the previous month as a black misery. She either felt the need to, or actually did, spend most of her time moping in bed. She had 'opted out of her being' for a few weeks. Then she came out of that and felt part of the universe again. There seems to be an almost bipolar quality about her, and she sometimes talks at length about her emotional life as if it were a universe in itself which it probably is for any of us. In this meeting she is the opposite, taking a restrained view of her companions, almost a relaxed, judgemental position, though never unkind. She is, therefore, as hard to assess as Eve, and there are similarities between them in terms of detachment simultaneously accompanied by passion; as if Buddhism had taken root in their psyches without telling them. Catherine is an attractive and interesting person and one could only wish she finds the place of contentment within herself, the place we all seek for ourselves. Sometimes she seems to be there, contented and expansive, but at others she seems to be on a rack of self-accusation and spiritual hunger.

**Stefan.** He never fails to discover a new crisis or epiphany in himself and his relationships. In this meeting he is, as usual, personal confessor to everyone, acutely perceiving every twist and turn of each of the assembled psyches. In addition, he talks at length about his own struggles, not always coherently and rarely consistently. He is a remarkable man, not least in the courage and determination he puts into his own life-journey. Trained as an engineer, he sometimes yields too easily to 'technological psychotherapy' where common sense might be more appropriate. In a sense, he looks for the miraculous cure, a messianic variety of healing which ordinary science or medicine fails to deliver. Alternative or spiritual healing also attracts him, as does a labyrinthine route to deep self-knowledge. Two themes seem to dominant in his discourses in this meeting. One is his own indecision (or perhaps rather his determination to make his own decision) on whether or not to accept triple bypass surgery for his heart; the other is the enormous significance of the inner **divine child.** These two concerns are intertwined for Stefan. As is 'essence'; he brought a book by A.H.Almaas, 'The Elixir of Enlightenment', for Ellen and Marcus to read - Stefan is a keen educator. But all these themes run together for Stefan. He brings a freshness and a courage to every situation. It may be hard to comprehend what he says sometimes, but there is no denying his intelligence, insight and deep morality. There is also the schizoid element, a condition he has battled with as well as lifelong health issues. His family, a son and a sister, primarily, engage him fully, often turbulently. His discourse in the meeting ranged all over these matters. But at the end it was impossible to remember quite where he had arrived after a long speech. Perhaps the most direct way of sensing Stefan's intent is to look at the brief summary on the cover of the 'Enlightenment' book:

*'Almaas discusses the values and shortcomings of spiritual training, and explores why an impasse may occur. He reveals how a precise understanding of your own personality can free inner resources so that your essential being can lead you toward enlightenment'*

This probably sums up Stefan's quest as well as anything could. It is also worth recalling that it was his emphasis on the divine child that made Marcus see new significance in his 'snapshots' and his painting. This is an example of the way in which Stefan achieves inspiration of others.

**Ellen.** She actually said very little in the meeting yet her presence was enough to give the group coherence and value. Asked about it afterwards she expressed surprise that anyone had beeen enriched by her presence. It is difficult to know what is happening in her psyche, especially for herself. She is now rather old, at 82, and has been through a series of physical and mental traumas. As an Enneagram Number Eight, as she often reminds people, she can't bear to be told what to do, nor can she stand being 'helpless'. Yet she is deeply committed to staying alive and, if possible, being happy. There are obvious conflicts in these ingredients. She is dependent on Marcus's help to a degree that exasperates her and she is excessively concerned for his welfare. The latter was characteristic of her before she became ill. Her physical problems may well have some psychological ingredient - when do they not? The fact is that people find her profoundly inspirational. She is seen as an extremely wise woman. Her comments are trenchant and prized by those who hear them. This adds to the mystery of her being and carries an indication of her essence, in the Almaas sense. Perhaps the key is that she is both unwell and brimming with rare energy. The human condition is writ large and clearly in her. She is a joyous sufferer and almost without egoic presumption. Her directness and honesty are beautiful to experience. She has written several fine books and created many fine paintings. But that is now in the past. She enjoys it when someone is thrilled by one of her books, yet has no need nor interest in writing any more. This withdrawal might seem perverse but it is simply a matter of knowing when something is finished. Her life goes on.

# Essay 14
# A Passion Spent

Marcus's Ideal Philosophy: *to develop an individual and collective practice that is essentially secular and non-theistic and that focuses on moral and creative behaviours rather than beliefs. The fundamental spiritual drive in this objective is to protect what is divine or sacred in the human being from the rigidity and coercion of religion. The aim is to liberate the sacred impulse in a person and encourage it to manifest in behavioural excellence, free from belief systems and devoted to the good and the beautiful. While non-theistic, it would be fervently transpersonal, and seeking to transcend without supernatural assumptions.*

## A Not Biography

This essay describes the most recent struggle for enlightenment in the long search by Marcus for some sense in his life. It is not in the least a biography, and it is not intended to put forward Marcus as anyone in any way important. It is really an 'everyman' story, in that it shows the persistent self-delusion that rules his and our existence. His loves and his friends and his ideas and his projects are not in themselves of any interest to anyone but Marcus. However, if this essay has any value it is that it may alert the reader to the infinite cunning of the egoic self, which tramples or subsumes everything in what it perceives as its path. Marcus, like so many products of higher education in the 'advanced' western culture, is both highly intelligent and rather blinkered. He is intuitive, imaginative and psychologically myopic. Perhaps he just lacks street-wisdom. It is little short of a miracle that circumstances have been kind enough to make him revise radically both his world-view and his daily practice. This essay attempts to trace the wandering route leading to the revelation.

### The Beast in the Pulpit

On the face of it, the subject of the essay is his long and bitter battle with religion. Any religion; all religions. He detests religion. He has loathed religion since childhood, a longer loathing even than his horror of the human species as a whole. Although, by Enneagram decree, he is a 'Reformer', that is a 'Perfectionist', out of love with himself and his world, he has always behaved as though he has perceived a fundamental truth about existence. All personalities do this, of course - it is the curse of the Enneagram. It could have gone the other way: Martin Luther hated mankind and adored his god, Marcus loves humankind in principle but loathes it in practice and denies any god's existence. A similar fetish in many ways, if different in trivial detail. At least Marcus has avoided maniacal religiosity. Like everyone in the world, Marcus thinks he has a vision of some truth or other, rather than merely an acquired predisposition to think and feel in certain prescribed ways. An habitual belief is, unfortunately, no substitute for a fully-informed thought. In Marcus's case he had never questioned his particular disposition to regard humanity as pretty dire in general and religion as its greatest malignity. At the same time he has always been an idealist and, however paradoxically, adores the highest manifestations of human love, creativity and non-doctrinal morality. This duality in him has also been a source of despair as he has never quite known which of his truths to believe, if either.

## His Double Vision

Now, however, the two world-views are hurtling into one another and Marcus is being transformed before his very own eyes. Such things don't usually happen all at once except in those rare moments in esoteric mysticism when it is supposed to be instantaneous. His duality must have started edging towards a personal monism quite early on, though he wouldn't have identified it in that way. What stages might be recognised in this evolution, if that is the right word for the fragile growth of personal wisdom as opposed to the crunching accidentalism of natural forces in creating and destroying species? When he was still very young, he struggled with school, family and church because their doctrines and foibles grated upon his dreamy romanticism. He felt, and was, an alien. Early sexual awakening, too, was a beautiful dawn chorus that deteriorated rapidly into the cawing horror of a rookery. He was drawn to female beauty and repelled by exploitative appetites, both his own and those of his girlfriends. His parental home was a prison as well as a sanctuary. His father's moods and his father's kitchen garden were both equivocal yodellings to the young Marcus's ears. He escaped much of his confusion by plant-hunting and became romantically drawn to botany. He succeeded as a student but fell into depression in the grinding emptiness of postgraduate research. A tired old fellow of twenty-three, he became an unlikely Air Force officer, and if there had been any promise of excitement in that, it was soon doused by the monotony of teaching cadets and by dwelling in that comfortable nursing-home called an officers' mess. Out in the world again, a married man of twenty-six, he once again followed an empty dream. He was trying to square his internal circle but merely broke himself on the wheel of commerce. Easily done: he thought he'd found the ideal blend of country life, work in a family business, and caring for his beloved plants. All three ingredients were rancid from the start. The dualism did for him again. Country life proved to be the battleground of competitive farming in flat, dull, monocrop fields, in which wild animals and plants were uniformly treated as pests: it was itself a mendacious dualism between starry-eyed conservative rural politics and savage, rapacious, greed. The family business was a dysfuctional failure, in a world as driven by rapacity as the farmers it served, and in which poor Marcus stoically attempted to serve the vague causes of science and conscience. It tore him apart, psychically. As for the plants, there were his two worlds still: in the fields the monoculture of cereals or 'roots' were like troops on the Somme, destined for a pointless death one way or another. In hedgerows, lakes and rivers dwelt the 'weeds' that went some way to feed his romantic affection

## Art to the Rescue

Then, in his crisis-ridden thirties, he discovered painting and agonised compassion. The painting had to be learned the hard way. Why painting? Why bother? What transpersonal spirit was he pursuing? It is hard to say, now, when he has become a fluent and successful artist. But at thirty-five it could seem merely to be escapism from his boring, testing, job. Even promotion up the management ladder didn't stop him. Why was he trying to emulate a sort of scholar-gypsy while disguised in a sharp business suit? Duality again? Or was he subconsciously searching for a deeper reality even while he repudiated the religious path? As for the agonised compassion, this was partly because he became interested in bird-watching. Why? It was presumably a resurrection of his plant-hunting youth. But despite the pleasures of the chase, it involved him in seeing for the first time what a bloodbath the world of nature actually is, notwithstanding the poet's ecstasy. This time, the duality consisted of his delight in walking in woods and hills with binoculars at the ready, while miserably mulling the transience of the lives of the feathered beauties.

## Middle-Age Megalomania

As he approached fifty, therefore, he melded his youthful dualities into one great binary mindset, and, dangerously for the peace and balance of his mind, there was in him, somewhere, the notion that he was the only person who could really see it. This is, of course, ideal Enneagram-One material. Here there is also a special variant of duality, interestingly, in which the mind judges the world harshly and even coldly, while the heart bleeds profusely for what the mind observes and deduces. Not unlike the suffering/ compassion of the non-attached Buddhist, a mindset he had yet to meet. At fifty, Marcus wrote his first book. He called it 'The Glass Pillar' and it was little more than a wordy justification for 'ignorance', or possibly, humility in the face of the unknowable. Big thoughts. Or so he thought. It was, at least, an attempt to nullify duality, to simplify his constant hopping from one foot to the other. But did it work? No, because he still aggrandised his own misery, even if it were now consistent through and through. But even that failed to happen. He just shifted the pattern of his duality. What did happen was that Marcus fell, for power and imfluence, monist enough one might think, except that he still held on to the seductive emotion of the see-saw. Down at a 'safe and hidden' level, now. He convinced himself that he was pursuing a path of enlightenment, because he was in love with that ideal. He began meditating and developed his taste for fine wine. He bought a seaside cottage. He was still miserable and irritable, usually at the same time. Dualism had now become a fierce conflict throughout his psyche, but a conflict immersed in hedonism.

### The Triple Trap

Each of the nine personality types hypothesised in the Enneagram has three manifestations. This proves nothing, nor is it proved, but it is an interesting theory: in the case of the Number One Type, Reformer/perfectionist, the suffering personality can shift either to Number Seven or Number Four.

The first is a 'good' displacement because the tight-arsed One can indulge in the pleasures of the ever-optimistic, enthusiastic Seven; the Epicure, or the tender miseries of the doleful, solipsisitic Four; the Tragic Romantic. It is a puzzle how Marcus's duality fits into this theoretical trinity. He certainly displays all three characterisations over a period of time. Maybe there are just two options in practice: One veering to Seven, or One veering to Four. Basically, then, Marcus may either be a perfectionist on a bender or a perfectionist in sackcloth and ashes. This fits Marcus, anyway. Either way, it is Marcus the Supreme, whether celebrant or self-flagellant. In practice, Marcus on a bender can be an irritating 'life and soul' of anyone's party, or he may be the singer, the orator, the comedian, the raconteur. He has always been attracted to performers, to actors, to charismatics (if non-religious). He loves to show-off. He remembers that his father needed to show off. It may be a genetic planning error. So, in a sense, the painting is also Marcus bendering. It may have been more than a mere indulgence to relieve the pain and monotony of his business life.

Also in practice. Marcus can also do a Savonarola, something Ellen often points out, acidly. The state of the planet has become an obsession of his as have many other features of the age: football arouses his negative passions as much as anything can. Either way, Marcus is a judge, comic or grave, and either way he is a man with a serious superiority complex. Or is he?

## The Crucifixion

The speed and ease with which Marcus can be discountenanced do not quite fit the 'superiority complex' theory. His is an extremely fragile confidence. He has recently recognised that during his eighty years he has suffered maybe five or six crises that could be called 'nervous breakdowns', or perhaps his life has been one long nervous breakdown with variations. Here is a subtler duality, perhaps, a contrast whereby a person may be overweening one minute and crushed the next. Or it may take a longer time. In business, for instance, which is now far into his past, Marcus was in despair and desolation when one of the operations under his general chairmanship behaved fraudulently. He couldn't cope with the shame and the fear in it. One of his colleagues had told him to 'stop crucifying' himself. But a big ego carries a big responsibility. Marcus collapsed under the burden and embraced responsibility for the failure in the small subsidiary. He could have shrugged it off, at least psychologically. But he couldn't. Instead, he did a spiritual, but still secular, resurrection.

## The First Books and Gurus

Marcus chose to pursue a spiritually elevated awareness in his late fifties. He brought and still brings to this venture all the psychological baggage he was theoretically seeking to ditch. This is the best part of the story, as it is where self-deception rides supreme. Well, maybe not quite supreme. Light seeps a little into the solid darkness of his deeper soul. It has been doing that, on and off, for years. To be fair to his aspirations. But only recently has the process become really dangerous for him. More is being illuminated than he could have imagined even as recently as a year or two past. But first, the story turns to the writing of books and the pursuit of gurus and guruhood. Marcus cherishes the spirit of atheism and derides the credulity of believers and the speciousness of priests. So much is fact. Yet he is devoted to the spiritual life, even to divinity, but entirely within the human ambit. There is no supreme being, at least not a friendly one. These things he knows. He consistently insists that he will only deal with non-religious spirituality. He puts it in his website. He is proud to be a spiritual nonbeliever. This is even translated into 'mystical atheist' in one of his later books. So, what was and is this new-found passion for writing? It waited until he was sixty-seven before it manifested itself as an actual book, seven years later than when he began seriously singing. The two activities were connected. Marcus was using his voice to tell the world something. The books were the main venture. Singing was hard for him because his voice, though fresh and undamaged by over-use, was getting old and struggled to fulfil the promise and carry out the exercises and learn the musicality demanded of it. Writing, however, flowed fairly easily through him, if not yet quite under his control. The first novel began with the objective of anatomising the Enneagram, having nine main characters each with the appropriate personality-format. There were nine chapters, one for each character but involving the other eight. The book soon took over the programme and drove towards a duality, two main characters, who would continue to struggle together for a further three novels. While Marcus acted out his own duality in the interaction of his two male characters in the 'Fairley Quartet', a title that referred to Marcus's home-town, he pursued a parallel search with 'real' people in various groups, with sundry gurus and 'masters'. This latter process, in various stages and forms, was to go on for two decades. In that time, he wrote further books, mostly on the theme of personal growth and opening awareness. This rather hectic activity, for a man in his seventies, may have caused his coronary attack. But other things contributed to a new journey, one which eventually led to something that could be seen as actual enlightenment.

### The Second Coming

In the second half of his seventies, Marcus gradually became aware of a deep malaise in himself. He had given up drinking and singing and focused upon reading and writing, still trying to find his way. He felt increasingly absurd: an old man in infant school. What was it that gnawed at him, making him search and search, as if there was some goal that had to be reached? Why did the groups now grate upon him, as people went round and round the carousel of mythical certainties? Why was he still so angry and afraid? (At least he figured out that he had these problems.) He knew he wanted serenity above all things, but serenity he just couldn't get. He needed something extra, something to jolt him into a different dimension or reality. He felt imprisoned in all the old assumptions. A move in this direction occurred as a result of studying the 'ox-herding pictures' in Buddhism and letting the message gradually sink in. He realised that it was a portrait of himself. Like the Chinese ox-chaser, Marcus had worked assiduously to become enlightened, or so he thought. He even tried to teach others about it. It was, he said, a parable about spiritual pride. And the process resulted in a great psychic crash, in the story, when the Void displaced everything. Gradually, for Marcus, the Void became the primary focus of his existence. People would ask him, 'What is this Void of yours?' He would explain that it was the source of everything, an emptiness containing the potential of everything. Incomprehension. Or: 'Oh, you mean God!' Not God, of course, because the Void was 'neutral, indifferent to humanity, just the source of everything with no intention'. That was how Marcus saw it. He pointed to Zen and Tao as spiritual philosophies that centred on the concept of the Void. Inevitably, he wrote about it, too. To a degree, Marcus was reborn. Some baggage-dropping had taken place. He was ready, though he didn't know it, for the next positive shipwreck.

### Unitarians Awake!

Ellen, who was on her own tired tiger, needed a community and took Marcus to the Chapel, his teeth gritted. Even that low-octane religiosity was hard for him to endure. But he liked the people. Some became good friends. Poetry and play-reading were incidental joys. Marcus discovered a new enthusiasm for writing. Then a cataclysm in the making. Partly inspired by Marcus, though by no means only him, there was a move to 're-think' the community. It was in this initiative that Marcus began to open his long-shut eyes. He thought, or assumed, that he knew better than everyone else how such a process should go forward. He saw himself as a grand strategist. He would guide the process. He tried to guide the process. At the centre of his philosophy lurked the lifelong hatred of religion and his ambition was to turn the Unitarian community into an entirely secular group. He tried to put this to his closest friends. There was an explosion. Cleo threw a grenade into his core. She said that he could think what he liked, as Unitarians did, but he should not try to change or deride anyone else's beliefs. He derided hers, she thought. He insisted that unless the Unitarians threw out all the God-stuff they could never move on. He quoted Christopher Hitchens. This was Marcus in full battle-order. This was the Marcus that Marcus had always failed to recognise. He could not have changed what he did not see.

### Seeing

Ironically, just as Marcus was getting treatment for cataracts and having his physical sight saved, he now saw an awful truth. His entire life had been dedicated to, and governed by, **power-lust.** He had exploded the myths of gods and the adoration of the self, he had exposed belief-systems as vainglorious idiocy, he had repudiated most human activities as the vicious play of children, and all the while he was consumed by an unrecognised obsession with personal power. It might be, and probably is, the basic psychology of all people, but it was a huge shock to Marcus to realise that he was obsessed with power. He had always rejected Ellen's worship of energy or anyone else's worship of some god or other, and here he was, lost in the worship of the most egregious of all natural phenomena, power. This he now saw. What does he now do? First, and maybe last, he has to downgrade all his previous assumptions to mere inclinations. His personal beliefs, which he denied possessing, and disguised and paraded as scepticism or ineluctable logic, needed to be eased into compassionate retirement. He has to let go of his power-need, doesn't he? Or he needs to transform it into something useful? Or pleasant, possibly beautiful? Is there a precedent that might guide him, as it would surely be arrogant of him to assume he can turn the dark tide of human evolution, single-handedly that is.

## The Power Illusion

As if anticipating his forthcoming fall into grace, Marcus painted a series of Cnut or Canute paintings. He started with a fine ironstone boulder alone on the beach at Sandsend near Whitby. It was a metaphor. This great stone was regularly engulfed by the sea and was gradually being eroded. But it didn't make great paintings. So Marcus changed each picture into an abstract-expressionist portrait of the old king. Here are two versions of the story of Canute's attempt to command the waters:

1. *Canute is famous for the tale of the incoming tide. According to legend, Canute's courtiers flattered him into believing that his word was so powerful that even the tide would recede at his command. Canute is said to have taken this compliment literally and had his throne placed by the*

*shore and vainly attempted to command the waves to recede until he almost drowned. An alternative version states that Canute was extremely wise and put on this practical demonstration to show his courtiers that he was not taken in by their flattery. The event is commemorated by a plaque at Bosham.*

*2. Henry of Huntingdon, the 12th-century chronicler, tells how Cnut set his throne by the sea shore and commanded the tide to halt and not wet his feet and robes. Yet, continuing to rise as usual, the tide dashed over his feet and legs without respect to his royal person. Then the king leapt backwards, saying: 'Let all men know how empty and worthless is the power of kings, for there is none worthy of the name, but He whom heaven, earth, and sea obey by eternal laws.' He then hung his gold crown on a crucifix, and never wore it again. This incident is usually misrepresented by popular commentators and politicians as an example of Cnut's arrogance.*

Well, which was it? Like Marcus's lifelong duality, here is egoic obsession with power in its two modes. There is also arrogance upon arrogance in the stories - and in Marcus. Arrogance 1 consists of the delusional belief that a powerful monarch is sufficiently backed by cosmic authority that any order will be obeyed. (Even in today's sceptical world, emperors such as Hirohito of Japan or Elizabeth 11 of England have a claim to divine authority; and Prince Charles of Wales and Cornwall believes he was put on earth to do great things.) All humankind have a touch of this, if it is only in the form of 'human rights'. Arrogance 2 is in the more secret certainty that other people are more deluded than one's (royal) self. So Canute and Marcus have this fall-back position in which they will say 'Oh, I knew that all along', when their hubris is exposed. This means that Marcus's revelation of his own power-lust can be swept away or under the carpet by various types of broom. The ultimate test is very deep in the psyche, probable beyond conscious access. If so, and surely it must be so, Marcus must watch himself in all his doing and being. It could be said that he should have been doing this for years, having worked so hard at his awareness and so assiduously in the dismantling of his huge false self. Of course he should, and he'd be the first to admit it, but the stain won't wash out so easily. It must be re-emphasised that Marcus is not in the least unique or special, although he could be if he succeeds in his new perception. But power lurks here, behind yet another tree in his Druidic grove. If he *did* manage to defeat the dragon of power-presumption, he'd be vulnerable to another chasm of arrogance, i.e. that he'd have become the first human being to achieve full freedom from the old Adam of congenital gracelessness. There seems to be a vast succession of Russian Dolls here, a complete and new theory, by which every new breakthrough in awareness is eaten by the one before, so that actual breakthrough in awareness never happens or is always provisional and transient. Is the position hopeless for Marcus?

## A Modest Resolution
Death being the only possible full resolution (unless

evolutionary reincarnation gets him by the gonads) for Marcus, and given that he likes living with Ellen et al, he must come to a realistic accommodation with his rampant power-ego. False modesty is out, for obvious reasons. So is self-abnegation. Scourging the body till it flows with blood is probably more show than substance. Maybe the only practical recourse is to become loving to all creatures, even human ones. A reassuringly difficult programme. He could almost allow himself to feel special if he managed it. But, fortunately, he couldn't.

### The Internal Mother

Mother Theresa is a popular prototype of the all-round lover of everything, Mother Meera is another. Are they signposts for the new Marcus? Could Marcus possibly become divinely motherly? If that's too big an ask, could he become divinely fatherly. Oh, God, we're back to God, are we? Painted into a corner? Divinely brotherly, then? Ask his actual brother or his brother-in-law if it is feasible? Come off it! Maybe 'motherly' it has to be, as it is the most unlikely scenario and it should keep him busy.

# Essay 15
# A Vision of Unity

## Storm in an Egg-Cup in Middlearth

In the realm of the Hobbitarians there was perturbation; a small but perfect storm in a tiny chalice. As in Tolkien's flawed masterpiece, the little people of Middle Earth, as he called it, were regarded as a model of common-sense and humility for normal human creatures of clumsy girth and hairless feet. In Middlearth, too, the non-Tolkien version, the Chief Hobbit was usually female. In this account she is Frodene, an ethereal little woman, with wonderful intentions but vague execution. The small enclave of Hobbitarians was not especially hard to govern, though the members of the tribe were always given to argument just for the pleasure of it. This meant that the role of Chief Hobbit was harder than it might seem superficially.

## Frodene's Dilemma

Part of her problem was her lack of pure breeding. She was not an original Hobbit. She had been raised in a different time-warp, a small and exquisite cult from far away Indonesia that had no connection with Hobbitarianism. She had, therefore, slightly off-centre qualities for the Middlearth people. She had an unfamiliar mixture of traits, which included an iron will encased in ethereality. She was also extremely musical, perfect in principle, but perhaps too good in practice for the down-to-earth hobbits. Her worst failing, if she has one, might be her unpredictability: the Hobbits must have predictability. Anyway, they had chosen her for their leader. Unfortunately, the main problem for Frodene, though she might not have realised it, was that none of the Hobbits could agree on what they wanted from their leader and much enjoyable argument was had on this question. More basic still was the delightful argument over whether the Hobbitarians wanted a leader of any kind. Perhaps they did and they didn't. Maybe they had one quality of ordinary humans: they wanted their leader-cake and eat it as well. Previous to Frodene was a leader who was just right. She is beyond compare for Hobbitarians. They cannot breathe her name out loud. She is like Yaweh to the ancient Judeans. She had embodied Hobbitarianism perfectly. Indeed, for the small enclave of some forty or fifty Hobbits in Middlearth, she had taken Hobbitarianism to a new level of congeniality. She had been completely dedicated and reliable. Her life had been devoted to Hobbitry. Then she had retired from the scene. Like any brilliant leader she had left her flock desolate and in disarray. They had become inured to the need for a leader. That may seem a negative way of putting it, but the fact is that she had been too effective as a leader and she had left them unprepared for self-governance. Still, there was a back-up in the Hobbitarian system, as there usually is for this wise, earthy, people. There was The Board of Practicality, usually called BOP. This body of elected Hobbits was responsible for the management of the enclave as distinct from the spiritual leadership of the Chief Hobbit. Regardless of written rules, the BOP and the Chief Hobbit were not easily distinguished in matters of great concern for the general Hobbitry. There was overlap and confusion, making great opportunities for enjoyable dispute. Not just enjoyable dispute, unfortunately. Occasionally, the Hobbit community became concerned with issues of power and glory, so that frivolous argument morphed into enraged quarrelling. And Hobbits do not quarrel well.

## The Battle of the BOP

Hobbitry is nothing if there is disunity. Hobbits have a sublime desire for tolerance so that there may be true unity. This formula is not entirely robust. It is blown apart by the first hint of a power-struggle. Necessarily. It is as if the immune-system of the enclave's organisation turns upon itself, devouring its own substance. How did this particular power-struggle rear its Medusa-head? How was it that neither the Chief Hobbit nor the hierarchy of the BOP could stop the slide into anarchy? How was Middlearth allowed to descend into civil war? A very small civil war, admittedly, and one that had no relevance for the big, real world looming beyond the tiny Eden of Middlearth, yet it represented the weakness at the heart of all good intentions. The sinister little rot in the heart of small-town Hobbitarianism was a local phenomenon yet it symbolised the global weakness of the human species, its inherent tendency to destroy itself and all around it. The Hobbits were vociferous in their criticism of wasteful wars and global pollution, yet here they were, on a Lilliputian scale, committing identical behavioural errors. One of the prime movers of this dispute was apparently motivated by genuine anxiety. He was a conscientious Hobbit who wanted

Hobbitry to make friends with everyone regardless of sect or creed. Like liberals in big politics, he wanted to do good in the world without any meanness of spirit. Who could quarrel with that? Well, another Hobbit, for one. She was a traditionalist, a conservative, a rule-observer, who feared the dangers of careless friendliness. She seemed to be protecting the Hobbit enclave from over-exposure to, or even exploitation by, outside forces. The clash of these molecular Titans made a shattering din. Other Hobbits lined up on either side. There were threats and resignations. There seemed no stopping the Gadarene route.

### Centripetal/Centrifugal

The anxious Hobbit who made the call to arms told others that he was taking a dialectical stand. There are always big words available to embroider mundane impulses. And why not? It makes life interesting. Yet it can lead us astray. An impartial and disinterested but interested observer might wish to say that the whole thing was baloney. Yes, you could argue that generous inclinations are the thesis, that cautious resistance is antithesis, and that the synthesis is the result of wise analysis. A coming together and resolving of differences. But no. As the observer might say, it is bullshit. What we have here, as in human affairs generally, is a bloody power struggle. In simple terms, you could also say that some power-impulses point outwards and some point inwards. Usually both at the same time. Centrifugal forces aim towards the outside edge, centripetal energy points inwards to the centre. It beats 'dialectical' doesn't it? But it's still bullshit. It's the human psyche we're looking at here. The Old Adam himself. Every human is motivated by desire, or the need for power, or both. Prime Ministers pretend, or more worryingly, believe, they are acting unconditionally and purely for 'all the people'. Oh Yeah? They really don't mind being toppled? Or topped? Pull the other one. They just want to win; to win everything, for ever. The thing about the Hobbitarians is that they sincerely want to be nice. Friendly and tolerant is what they want to be. And our observer may come close to believing them. They really did seem to mean it. And even if it was really all for themselves, no problem: if they behaved like saints who is to argue? Now, in disarray, they ought to hunker down and re-think themselves from the semi-conscious upwards.

## The Vision Thing

So let's imagine that they sit down together and work it all out. The observer confesses to mystical eccentricity from the start, but something lies unacknowledged in his scattered psyche. Sure there are Hobbitarians, here, playing power politics with centripetal and centrifugal policies, which should not matter in a balanced little universe but something darker lurks in them. Think instead, as the observer must, of *egopetal* and *egofugal* as the real forces throwing the Hobbits into terminal confusion. The observer is not innocent. Indeed, he fancies himself as a **seer,** seeing into the future in an intuitive but bogus way. Maybe not quite bogus. Trends can be read, suspicions engendered, scenarios imagined. But in his fancy he is something special. Someone special. At the first sniff of a planning opportunity, he is up and running, tail wagging, nostrils flaring. Round and round he goes, ego pulling and pushing, in and out, puffing vigorously with the transcendental energy of managed karma. So, while the small Titans in the Hobbit POM, led but not led by the chairhobbit, dance along their suicidal radii, he is on his Hobbitarian seesaw too, creating a future out of thin and rancid air. The landscape shifts, dissolves, reshapes itself. Power is unleashed beyond understanding. There is madness on the Hobbitarianismic earth. A madness composed of unregenerate and atavistic longing to control. This is how change asserts itself, besides and usually despite, Hobbitarian intent. First the observer looks upon his own conversion. He see theirs when he sees his own, which is the knowing that yet another piece of his supposed being is discarding itself.

## A Shifting Template

What is the true personality? Where is this truly true self? Isn't it taken for granted that what we are is what we were somehow 'meant' to be? Now, in the security of science, we can blame the genes, though even now many of us think ourselves fashioned by Almighty Hands. We carry an ego bravely; we know we have to have one, but it seems to be a mixed blessing, good for getting ahead, bad for sweet humility. These are our stories. They are also the Hobbitarian stories: it seems the same narrative in most tribes, one way or another. So sure are we of our provenance that we speak convincingly of human rights and the sanctity of (human) life. For the observer, a new man that once called himself a seer, this story is at best garbled and at worst plainly and absolutely false. This basic, fundamental, human self-image, the Hobbitian self-image, and most particularly his own self-image, is a lie. Not, unfortunately, a conscious lie as is that of the ordinary con-man or snake-oil salesman. This lie is deep and hidden. It must be approached cautiously or it will evade him, or transmute into false innocence. The automatic pilot of man and hobbit is undeclared self-importance. When the observer says that he wants to be respected, or his works acknowledged, or his opinions listened to, he is living the lie. He may get away with it because all of us have the same lie. Until now, he thought that its prevalence made it harmless, that we all cancelled out each others' egotism. This is also a lie. He was wrong in this assumption. The lie is a cosmic immorality. The lie is because we really know it all already. We have all lived with it. We pretended that we knew what was what in the human jungle. Not so, dear seer. The idea that we are all born in sin is a get-out clause. Useful but iniquitous. Not true, we do not have original sin, we produce it in our psychic factories as we go along.

## I Am A Hobbit

What is he saying? That he is ordinary? Yes. That he is a minute speck in the Great Continuity? Yes. We are all Hobbitarians, whatever other fancy names we give ourselves. And like the Hobbits of Tolkien we are in great danger, though not from a Dark Lord, or a Light Lord, but from our own absurd pretensions. This is also what we are. A danger to ourselves. We threaten ourselves with manic preciousness.

That damnable ring that we fight each other to possess. The Ring of Power. This problem of power is at the root of human suffering. We are afraid of losing it. We are afraid of gaining it. Is that not true of every one of us? How can we live together without the contamination of power? How do Hobbitarians show their flag of joyous powerlessness? How do they fly it? How do they identify it? Once he worshipped the Tyger burning bright in the forests of the night. Such power was there. He was the Tyger without knowing it. Self-empowerment is an easy option if you have enough imagination and self-deceit.

### And so to Tao

Tao is the supreme Hobbitarianism. Take number 37 (Mitchell translation):

*The Tao never does anything, yet through it all things are done. If powerful men and women could centre themselves in it, the whole world would be transformed by itself, in its natural rhythms. People would be content with their simple, everyday lives, in harmony, and free of desire.*

*Where there is no desire, all things are at peace.*

Frodene, like the impotent Dalai Lama, was struggling with non-power and we marvel at their patience and fortitude. But Hobbits and Tibetans crave for action, for some idea of freedom. So does the partial, impartial observer. We want the world to become good. We want the world to give us what we want. It is a Tibetan Hobbit's human right. This is the root of the big lie. Our big lie. As it was until the day before yesterday. We are only ten thousand years old and have much to learn. At least and maybe at last maybe we can recognise the lie. Despite scepticism, atheism, and poetic logicality, our observer was fooling himself. He thought he mattered. Yet he does not. Not at all. No more than the demented blackbird acrobatically attacking the suet balls hanging on a branch in a patio. Think of the Tibetan protesters festooning themselves with barbed wire to repel helpers while they burn in a hellish ball of suicidal fire. This is an unbearably powerful act of self-importance. In the act of agonised self-immolation there is total power over the universe. Suicide is an act of revenge upon the cosmos. We are not so brave. But just as insane. We have lived a life-time devoted to exerting power. Most often we are unaware of what we're was doing. Now we can know. What can we do? Think of Frodene in her hot seat.

## Frodene's Tao

The power of her predecessor, like that of my ancestors and culture, was the Mess of Pottage that makes the trivial seem important and destroys true value. Bilbonella was a great leader. She could have commanded an army. Bilbonella understood power and was an intelligent purveyor of it. That is the Mess of Pottage that the Hobbitarians are trying to digest. They are bingeing on trivia. It will probably pass. There will be some vomiting. But Hobbitarianism won't necessarily go down the pan as well. Whatever the Dalai Lama does or does not do, the mountains of Tibet will continue to glower in the icy mist. The problem lies in the lies. Frodene, and each of the other Hobbits, and the mad seer too, face the moment of the day over and over, always different, always the same, the moving nowness which has to be lived. So the question is: can we find truth within the mess of lies?

## Spirit of Spacetime

As for the observer, mystic and poet, he lives and loves in spacetime. It is all that saves him from the madness of egotism and the monstrous nagging of power. This spacetime, this continuum of all, is **spirituality**. He keeps on saying that the Hobbitarians, like the Humanistians, the adjacent tribe, lack spirituality, though he hasn't been very clear what he means. Now he begins to know. The missing spirituality is in the Tao, for one example. And in Zen. And lingeringly in bits of the big religions. And in the imagination of some scientists. And in mysticism. And in meditation. And in the natural world. It is everywhere and no particular where. Spirituality is easily confounded, destroyed in a moment's foolishness. It can be hard work to retrieve it. Spirituality is not resident in rules, policies, systems, creeds, and doctrines; spirituality is negated by any belief and any belief-system. Spirituality is spacetime in action, completely free, utterly unpredictable, and beyond mere human comprehension. Love, compassion, empathy, curiosity, friendship, kindness, and creativity, may all be touched by spirituality, but that is never guaranteed. Spirituality does not dwell in an egg-cup occupied by a storm. But maybe it can be found in a holy chalice untouched by doctrine.

# Essay 16
## Sextet on a Sunday Afternoon

*Cast*

Carrie, not escaping the burden of her Mother. Eliza, recovering neither memory nor authority. Ellen, recovering neither mobility nor self-regard. Eve, perhaps recovering after death of Adam. Marcus, trying to put down the burden of belief. Stefan, apparently recovering after heart surgery.

### Mid-afternoon in a sunny conservatory in May.

*All assembled except Stefan. He enters smiling and confident, though with the air of a man who has been through an immense experience. Everyone focuses on him. He is being assessed for signs of genuine well-being. There is a collective sigh of relief as it becomes clear that he is actually quite well.*

**Ellen and Carrie** (speaking almost in synchronised duet). It's really marvellous to see you, Stefan, and looking so well too. It's amazing. You did have the operation, didn't you? You've lost weight, too…

**Stefan.** Aye, I bloody did and I bloody have - a stone - but the crew were marvellous, the drugs were brilliant, and I were in top form when I come round. My voice was real strong. I could feel its strength in me…

**Marcus**. I was astonished when you rang me that evening, and it's true, your voice was extremely powerful. The whole thing is amazing…

**Stefan.** Aye, but, I have to say it was the only part that was. Everything else in me was weak. I felt bloody empty.

Just nothing there. At all. And I had to sort meself out on the medication. A few days went by and I thought, why the hell am I taking all this stuff? I thought: what I need is normality, normal food, natural recovery not all these bloody drugs. But don't get me wrong. The drugs have got their uses. The operation went like a dream; in fact it was a dream. Really. Anyway, I stopped all the medication. I told me doctor that was it, no more pills and potions, me body, I said, was telling me what to do and I believed what it was saying and he said OK. He understood. And I was right. Because I am getting better. Better than before, obviously. But they did a good job. Look: *(Stefan pulls up his shirt to show the scar down his sternum and then pulls up his trouser-leg to show the long scar where the blood-vessels had been extracted)*

**Eve** (knitting). They are beautiful scars. What a wonderful job they have done.

**Marcus** (Sightly aghast at the sight of the wool and needles). What are you knitting, Eve? Or, rather, why are you knitting, Eve?

**Eve.** A sock. I am trying to get into my Five.

**Stefan** (laughing). But you don't have a Five. Yours are Four and Eight. Or do you mean the Five of the Eight?

**Eve** (smugly). Yes, that's it. I want to be an observer today.

**Eliza** (eyes wide and angry). What on earth are they talking about?

**Ellen** (gently). Just the Enneagram. Don't you remember, Eliza? Each type has two sub-types, depending on degree of stress. Eve is being a bit free and easy, using a subtype from a different type... Five is the recessive sub-type of Eight not Two... you're an Eight, like me, and it is us who have the Five as a hideaway place.

**Eliza.** So Eve is hiding away by knitting? What is she hiding away from? Us? We're not worth hiding away from. We're just sad people, aren't we?

**Eve.** I am not hiding from you. Nor from myself. I just need some rest. Maybe I am hiding a bit from life. Maybe that. A rest from life, yes?

**Ellen.** Oh, a rest from life. Not death, surely not that. But a rest from fear and frustration. I have done such damage to myself in the past. And now I'm not eating enough. I am only seven stone, now. How do I get a rest from all this?

**Carrie.** Let's go round the group and see where we all are. Let's meditate first.

**Stefan.** Meditate on hiding away. Resting. Renewing, perhaps.

(The stage is silent for a few minutes. The cast shut their eyes. Except Marcus, who studies each of the other five. Then he also shuts his eyes. They become awake to the sound of sobs from Carrie.)

**Carrie.** Sorry. I just kept seeing the face of my mother. She's so petty. And bloody angry. And unfair. Why do old people misbehave so badly?

**Marcus.** Do we? Do you behave badly Ellen? And you, Eliza? You know, Carrie, the three of us are 250 years between us. Such wisdom, eh? You're so lucky to have us, you three youngsters. And are we not beautifully behaved? Look at us, now, models of propriety. So what do you mean, young Carrie?

**Carrie** (ignoring Marcus, who sits grinning amiably at her). Is it childishness? I mean is my mother visiting her infantility? Is she losing her understanding of adult existence? It's not bound to last after all. So I couldn't hold it against her, could I?

**Eliza.** It's probably a control issue. For your mother, I mean. She's probably feeling worthless. That's the big thing of old age. There's this feeling of being no use at all. Endless reassurance is needed when you are old.

**Stefan.** Yeah, it's real hard to own the needy side of oneself. And that's not just the old 'uns. It gets to be a conspiracy. Where are you in this, Carrie? Yes, I know you feel you've gotta be there for her, but not all the time. And when there's a third person, your sister for example, you can have the Third Person Syndrome, where this third person can make the behaviour worse. I reckon you've just gotta accept the downright silliness of your mother. Stop taking it personally. Not your fault. Don't be ashamed for her. Above everything, don't, don't, don't be hurt by her daftness.

**Carrie.** So do we forget all about fairness? Do we just let go of the concept of justice in human relationships? Surely not. So I am certainly hurt by the injustice of my mother. I don't deserve it. Well, do I?

**Stefan.** My turn, I see. Well, I've had my turn, really, with me heart and medications and all. But this justice thing is interesting. At the microcosmic level, like here and now, we need justice and will play hell to get it. The amount of time and money and blood that's wasted on microcosmic justice is massive and getting worse. Workers' rights. Human rights. Animal rights. Compensation. Prisons. Police. Laws and lawyers. Armies. Democracy. Aid. Sanctions. Embargos. You bloody name it. All nonsense. A quick check on the macrocosmos tells you that justice is a joke. It's just bloody pointless to even think about injustice. It is endemic in existence. Of course it is. What do you think drives evolution. Survival of the fittest. How unjust is that?

(There is silence in the group as Stefan's diatribe sinks in. Stefan and Carrie go out together rolling cigarettes. Marcus gets coffee for Ellen. Eve gets tea for herself and Eliza. While they drink, waiting for the smokers to come back, they discuss the full moon and its possible effects on human life. Ellen and Eve are pro-moon, believing it to exert major effects on the mind and emotions, Marcus and Eliza are moon-sceptics, though they accept the poetic power upon the imagination.

**Eve.** It is clear, I think, that something strong enough to move the oceans must exert great power on the water in the human body. The body is 80% water, and it cannot ignore the moon.

**Marcus.** Does a full moon change the effect of homeopathic remedies, too?

**Ellen.** Stop that, Marcus. Don't be so destructive of people's beliefs.

**Marcus**. When I was a botany student I was told that *Fucus* in a lab dish would ovulate at full moon to catch high tide fertilisation-potential. I took that as gospel, assuming that someone had actually monitored the seaweed on the laboratory bench. I was in the science faculty after all. Now supposing one of the lecturers had not done the work or seen the experiments yet dogmatically pronounced that seaweed sex organs were activated at high tide in a sea a hundred miles away, then it would have merely been a belief system and I would have been an idiot not to ask to see the evidence. So, far from being destructive to people's belief systems I am merely being practical. Otherwise I could accept any old bullshit.

**Ellen.** Did you really believe that stuff about seaweed ovulation. I reckon you were being sent up. I was in that department too and I don't remember that story.

**Marcus.** But would you have believed it?

**Ellen**. Probably not. It sounds a bit far-fetched.

**Marcus.** Well, there you are, then.

(Stefan and Carrie re-enter and Stefan asks what was 'far-fetched'.)

**Eliza.** Ellen and Marcus were discussing seaweed and the idea that it ovulates at high tide even if nowhere near the sea. I wonder if I ovulated at high tide when I lived in Bournemouth.

**Marcus.** Not relevant. The question is whether you ovulated at high tide when you lived in Birmingham.

**Carrie.** But she's not a seaweed.

**Marcus**. Too many variables. Human females left the sea a long time ago. But it could be interesting to investigate sea animals.

**Ellen.** I don't care. I want to talk about me. It's my turn.

**Marcus.** That's only because you haven't ovulated for a quarter of a century. (Marcus is told to shut up by the rest of the sextet and Ellen takes her turn, after a malevolent glare at Marcus.)

**Ellen.** I am still suffering from the side-effects of Citalopram. I can't walk as well as I did, and that was pretty bad anyway. I am more or less blind at times - and I happened to have a routine ophthalmic check-up just before I started the bloody medication and my eyes had not changed in a year. Also I can't really take in the bit I can read. Oh everything has gone wrong. I am really furious about it . . .

**Stefan**. Why did you start it? I am personally really pissed off with drugs generally. It seems madness to me that you should have done this to yourself. What the hell was the doctor up to?

**Ellen.** I wanted to stop being frightened all the time. I thought if I could reduce my anxiety I'd be able to get on with what's left of my life. And I felt so useless, too, so I hoped the medication would normalise me so that I could function properly. Instead, it's had the opposite effect. All I have left is being in groups like this, where I feel more or less alive and interested.

**Stefan.** That's really sad. I mean, you used to give away your energy to make other people well, and that was good work, if exhausting. I know how that feels. You could use it for yourself now. You should use it for yourself now. But you feel bewildered by all the things that have happened to you, don't you? What is stopping you from just getting it all bloody sorted?

**Ellen.** I know. I am absolutely frustrated with myself. I used to be ordered about from morning to night and I think I got into the habit of listening for instructions so that I had a chance of doing it right. But now I don't want instructions. But I haven't got freedom either.

(Stefan is transfixed by Ellen's situation. He evidently wants desperately to help but is afraid of making things worse for her. He goes to her and holds her hand. They sit silently for a while. No-one else speaks. The moment speaks for itself. Then Eliza moves forward and holds Ellen's other hand. Eliza starts to speak very quietly.)

**Eliza.** It's all those past scenarios. All that dead time and all those dead bodies. You and I can't bear to be told what to do, yet we always try to do what we think people want us to do. It's impossible. Mind-blowing. You and I are Eights. We lose our wits if we are actually ordered about. Our wits then stay unstable for fear of not getting it right.

**Ellen.** So what do we do about it? Is there an answer?

**Eliza.** Yes. Uniqueness. As each of us is quite unique, so is our future. Your future is unique. That's the answer. You just go for your own unique future without fear. That's your doorway. It's wonderful actually.

**Ellen** (Looking particularly at Marcus, her life-long partner). I'm going to need a lot of help to have any chance of achieving that. I can hardly believe it is possible. But there is nothing else to be done. I will try. Once I have left Citalopram behind I will make a fresh start. That is a solemn promise to myself.

(She releases her hands, thanks Stefan and turns to Eliza)

**Ellen.** Thank you for that Eliza, it's your turn now.

**Eliza.** I don't know where to begin because the record

turns continuously and always makes the same sound, a kind of pointless bloody wail, which is absolutely appropriate. I find myself shouting, 'Don't fucking well do that!' But I'm not sure if it comes out. Maybe it's just an internal scream. Anyway, there she is, doing it. Just bloody doing it. My house. My money. But she's the effing boss. I might as well not be there.

**Ellen.** Didn't the list work at all?

(Eliza looks blank. She turns her head rapidly, first left then right, as if seeking directions. Her face collapses into a drooping mask of misery. Her hands clasp and unclasp. She seems about to get up and run for it.)

**Eve.** You said you would give her a list of the jobs that you wanted done, and no funny business. It is your house, after all. She has to do your bidding. That is only right. You must insist.

**Eliza.** Maybe I forgot. Or perhaps I did. It is hard not to control your own house. I don't feel that I own it now. But it's getting a bit better, so I must have done a list. Yes, thinking about it, there is an improvement. Perhaps the problem is being resolved. The message may be filtering through. Oh that would be wonderful. It's horrible. I don't like feeling I could murder her.

**Stefan.** It sounds like you've got a major control-issue -we Eights are all the same we have to be in control and are buggered if anybody tries to control us. Have you spent the whole of your life, like me, with a 'put-down' syndrome, your life being characterised by being side-lined, of no particular significance…?

(Stefan is about to go off on a rant, which he does well, but Ellen and Eliza, fellow-'controllers', won't let him. They sing.

**Ellen and Eliza.** *'Don't know why, there aint no sun up in the sky, stormy weather, since my guy and I got together, it's rainin all the time . . . . '*

**Carrie.** I dreamt about Sylvia Plath last night. She was a stormy weather girl and had a stormy weather man, didn't she. I bet she was an Eight, too. Christ, what a bloody hellhole that relationship was! Who was to blame, d'you think?

**Marcus.** Does there have to be someone to blame in a relationship made in hell? The first thing she did when she was introduced to him in a party was to bite him in the face. A good start, don't you agree? I mean, you know where you are with a woman like that, don't you?

**Eve.** Ah, but they were poets. Poets are a different species. I am very interested in poets and I think they are extremely highly evolved and also very close to our atavistic roots. You know, transcendent and primitive at the same time?

**Carrie.** After that, I need a fag. Come on Stef, let's go and blow the weed.

(While they are out, the remaining four focus on the problems of a social creature. It is Eve's 'turn' and she picks up Carrie's theme of the 'ungracious old'.)

**Eve.** This is good for me. I am learning about my predicament. I am being hurt by Adam's mother. She is a difficult woman and Adam had to try very hard to stay calm with her. I am less successful than he was. And she makes me very childish, which is extremely upsetting considering how much work I have done on the maturing process. To hear

Carrie and Eliza protest about the people who bug them gives me both respite and insight.

**Marcus.** Tell us the insight, Eve. I mean, is this something about you or about others or life generally?

**Eve.** Oh well, not much I suppose, just a realising that I am now in alien territory. New to me because I am now alone in it.

**Marcus.** Part of the grief process? Without Adam to share reality with you reality has changed?

**Eve.** That is very good, Marcus. Yes. A whole new world with questions of how or where do I belong. I go miles to see Adam's mother and all she can do is to complain about the lumps in the porage I have made for her. I do not make lumpy porage. I make good porage. But for her the porage is lumpy.

**Ellen.** Silly old biddy. Presumably she's half-senile? To fuss about porage when she should be comforting you and being comforted by you! It has to be senility.

**Marcus.** Not necessarily. Maybe she is seriously disturbed emotionally. But tell me, Eve, how is the organist problem going? Has she stopped making her hideous racket yet?

**Eve.** I did not think of talking about that. But it is serious for me. There is this edgy balance between being truthful and being respectful. She is an awful organist. Adam so wanted to get a good organist. We suffered for twenty years from her racket. But if she lost the organist-role she would be both desolate and fatally hurt I am sure. She is also a Pooh-bah. She does everything. I would love to talk to her and understand her motivation. But how could I do that?

**Marcus.** Why don't you just leave. If anyone asks why, the answer is, 'I just can't take any more'. If that is the true position why not? Adam was the reason for your being there. You are now free to do as you please, aren't you?

**Eve.** Thanks. Really thanks. Let's leave it there. I will think on it.

(The smokers return and are unaware that they have missed Eve's turn. The sextet turns to Marcus.)

**Marcus.** All I have to share with you is my belief-crisis and I think you will not want to know it.

**Stefan.** What do you mean, 'belief-crisis'? (It isn't clear if Stefan is cross about the idea. He could be just very interested.)

**Ellen.** It's his bloody belief-system, Stefan. He claims to have no belief at all. But that's the biggest, most egoic belief-system of all. He is second-guessing all human experience and it makes me mad.

**Stefan.** She could have a point there, Marcus. Aren't you just being judgemental of everybody else? The others are nodding their heads. I reckon we all feel that you are being arrogantly judgemental.

(Marcus looks extremely angry, if a red face and a heavy frown and an absorbed stare at the floor constitute the symptoms of anger.)

**Ellen.** Come on Marcus. As an Enneagram One you are a real anger type. Lighten up. We all love you despite your arrogance.

**Eve.** I'm not sure about that. What Stefan said, I mean. Isn't the question whether or not you have the right to judge other people's beliefs and isn't your answer that you certainly do have the right to question anything and everything?

**Ellen.** If so, and I think it is so, then he does not have that right. The most he should do is to refrain from making any judgement. The only appropriate response to a belief that you don't share is to respond non-judgementally.

**Stefan.** This seems to be mainly a domestic issue between two people who have been married and arguing for nearly sixty years. I certainly find it more and more appealing to jettison all bloody beliefs, indiscriminately too.

**Marcus.** Is it OK if I say something? I haven't said much up to now. Nothing, in fact. Did I hear that right, Stefan? I've always thought of you as a person bursting with beliefs. What's happened? Is it the bypass?

**Stefan.** Aye, could be. I am bypassing my belief-blockages, eh? No, just go on Marcus and tell us what's goin' on for you.

(Marcus looks at Ellen with a sad expression. He needs her approval. Back to Stefan, his gaze is steadier. Then he studies the other faces. It is as if he is seeking permission for his anarchic concepts. This argument has happened before.)

**Marcus.** Well, I have to insist on being judgemental as a right and a necessity. It's mad to suppose that people's belief-systems are sacrosanct. Of course they must be challenged, but, I admit that I have had this wrong; I mean that I have made the wrong case or made the right case wrongly. I can understand Ellen's exasperation with me now that I realise my mistake.

**Ellen.** I wish you'd make up your mind for once. Do you damn all beliefs or not?

**Marcus.** In practice, I think I do, more or less. But that's only because most beliefs are crap. No, hang on, let me say it. My mistake was to say that all beliefs are crap because that is itself a ludicrous belief. You're right about that and I apologise for the muddle. This is where the judgement comes in. Your mistake, Ellen, is to say that all beliefs are valid and a matter for the individual. You say we should not pass judgement on other people's beliefs. I argue that it is morally and socially essential that we do just that. Judgement is vital, folks, do not hesitate to make it.

(The other five characters all shout at the same time. Marcus has hit a nerve. Intentionally, of course. Marcus is a pedagogue. He is smiling. He knows something important. He waits for the hubbub to die down.)

**Marcus.** Now, here goes. I so want you all to see this. It's not a matter merely of believing or not believing, which is no different from choosing the lamb or the beef on the menu. That's just emotional or constitutional preference. I may prefer to be a Catholic or an Atheist, and that's OK, so long as I don't expect anyone else to share my taste. But believing in a Catholic God, or believing there is no God at all, is a matter of great social and psychological significance. Being a belief it invites others to accept or reject it (unless it is kept secret, of course, in which case other complications come in.) The issue then becomes: is the evidence for the belief overwhelming? Is the 'truth' stated in the belief inescapable? I am proposing an Inescapability Test for all putative beliefs. That is all. If it is inescapable then it is a justified belief. If it is not inescapable it is not a valid belief and must be exposed as a mere preference or opinion.

**Ellen.** A bit of a rant, Marcus, but I get your point and I think I can buy into it.

**Eliza.** So what would be a belief, Marcus, in this system? How would it work?

**Carrie.** It wouldn't work because you couldn't prove this inescapability thing. If I say I believe that my mother hates me, how could that be proved either way?

**Stefan.** No, he's right on this, Carrie. Your belief that your mother hates you can either be shown as inescapable or it can't. If you can't find overwhelming evidence of it then it's just your opinion. No-one could deny your opinion. It just wouldn't have the status of a belief.

**Eve.** Why does any of this matter? Belief or opinion, who cares?

**Marcus.** It matters cosmically, Eve. Say I am a believer in the divine right of kings. No, seriously, it even has some currency in the modern age. I bet Charles of Wales thinks himself specially chosen by God to do things to us or for us. He has actually said as much. Well, it could matter terribly in a country or a time in which obedience to the monarch was considered absolutely necessary - a matter of absolute belief. Nowadays we can probably explode that nonsense in a second. Even though our constitutional monarch seems to believe she might be absolutely special only an idiot could agree with her. But just imagine trying to exist in a society where a belief in divine right was operative.

**Eve.** But you couldn't disprove it and survive. So what's the use?

**Marcus.** Yes, perhaps. But at least it is disprovable and was disproved. We are free of it, relatively, today because it could be disproved. It was not a belief, only an opinion.

**Eliza.** I still don't see that this is practically important in an everyday sense.

**Stefan.** The practical value of the inescapability test is that we can have a huge increase in tolerance. I am going home now, because I am tired. And I'm going to think about all the things I don't have to take on board because they are just matters of opinion. That's freedom, folks.

**Ellen.** If you can stand it.

**Carrie.** I think it could be pretty bloody terrifying, actually.

*(The sextet separates out into the constituent characters. There are hugs and kisses. Then Ellen and Marcus are left alone on the sunlit patio. They look old and tired. But they are smiling at each other. Something good has happened.)*

# Essay 17
# Internal Dialogue in a Bad Year

I am anyone and no-one. But I am perplexed and angry. That's me: Perplexed and Angry Esq., England, June, 2012. So far, it is being a bad year. For anyone. ('No-one' meaning merely anonymous and wishing to remain so.) For *everyone*, then, even if they are not aware of it, as most of them aren't. This is the tipping-point year, almost certainly. It is the tipping-point for me personally, and this Dialogue is about me too, as my anonymous beloved knows. She will need to know what I say here about my anonymous and questionable self. Apart from all the general stuff. Which she already knows after sixty years of our partnership.

**Tipping-Point Categories. A summary of the types of tipping-points operating in England today are:**

1. **Misuse of the Planet.** There can be little doubt that we have misused and are misusing this lovely planet. How dare we? We are not going to behave well. The tipping-point here is the catastrophic onset of absurdly high human population figures, and the degradation of the planet by over-use and misuse of 'resources' (a loaded word indeed.) This year marks the death of serious attempts to stop the rot. The Titanic Earth is starting to sink without lifeboats.

2. **Understanding the Universe.** We don't, we can't, and we won't understand the universe nor the multiverse, as Hawking now calls it. It is beyond our comprehension and Hawking's latest book, *The Grand Design,* shows why.

Optimism about finding 'answers', once the province of long-redundant religion, has now died in Science as well. We, as a species, are alone and ignorant as well as doomed. That's how it looks in mid-2012. Any convincing refutations? Is there really much potential in the search for practical survival over the next few years?

3. **Romanticising Nature.** A bit the same as the above, but the failure to see what nature is really like has continued to falsify reality in the same way as delusions about a loving, human-focused, deity. The two delusions fuse when catastrophes strike, large-scale or small. But the current experience may be just starting to teach us how wrong we are. Everything is going wrong, it seems, i.e. nature is behaving normally and screwing us as part of its normal practice.

4. **Hope and Meaning.** More human foolishness, based upon an ingrained assumption that our species has a special value. It goes with crazy ideas of divinity. There is also the great swathe of beliefs in general, actually concreted desires or fears, elevated to false positions. A spectral anxiety has begun to stalk the land of Britain, not before time. We are in deep trouble financially and in resource-availability. The same old optimistic slogans still appear here and there, but the discontent is burgeoning. We can't quite believe we are going down. Of course not. Britain rules the waves. Doesn't it?

5. **Leadership and Triviality.** It is strange what kinds of comforts Britons, and other races (the few not murdering each other), choose in hard times. The idea of leadership,

the hope that a messiah or a genius will come and save us, still unhinges us. Politics continue to wave this inane banner, there is a banal pretence that problems can be solved by strong decision-makers. Nonsense. But only now, this year, is there the slight possibility surfacing that leadership is fatally stricken. The truth is hidden by fatuous activity. The 'jubilee' of a fading, futile monarch, the preposterous aggrandising of celebrities, the rampant idiocy of the 'Olympics'. The incredible obsession with 'sport', above and below all, football. What is the tipping-point here? It is dual: on the one hand the decline is huge and rapid, on the other, the frenetic cheering and idolising is out of control. The two must collide somehow, somewhere, and there could be a mother of all revolutions.

6. **Knowledge and Chaos.** Faced with chaos the human mind creates the placebo, knowledge. Chaos is castigated as the one thing to be avoided and knowledge is the means of keeping the mad dog on a leash. This simplistic dualism is sliding down the same slippery slope as religion and science, or perhaps knowledge is sliding down as chaos slides upwards to replace it. The tipping-point is the slow, uneasy recognition that chaos is natural and real, as well as inevitable, whereas knowledge, for all its positive publicity, is a dangerous commodity.

7. **My Own Tipping-Point (Personal Importance** is tipping over for me. How about you out there? All seven billion personal importances. And that's just the human egoists. **The tipping-point is the realisation that the only thing I can change is me**.)

## Personal Importance (Pi).

The reality is, but never until now admitted, that I have always wanted to live in an Ivory Tower. All mod cons, of course, and optimum hedonistic opportunity. In that tower I would be impregnable yet free to judge and criticise the world outside, on which I would be superbly well-informed. The world would be submissively grateful for my attention and decisions. I would indulge in tantrums at the slightest hint of criticism of myself. I would, of necessity, be well-loved, well-paid, and held in the highest esteem. My judgement on myself would be harsh within the walls of the Tower. My reserves of righteous anger would be divided between the world and myself, my rage being rather more towards myself than externally directed. My pleasures would be diverse: wine, food, female love, passion, and companionship, the whole gamut of nature, creativity, entertainment, and above all the freedom to castigate idiocy, as I saw it, based upon religion, monarchy, patriotism, class, heritage, history, tradition, ballet, theatrical farce and musicals, travel, pop music, sport (especially sport), tribe, family, duty, guilt, pride, romance, and the entire edifice of scientific complacency. I could go on. But I will not. As sufficient is now said to show how abhorrent is this spectrum of personhood. The point being tipped here is twofold. On the one hand is the largely unrecognised monstrosity of my own Pi and, on the other, the possibility that I am not in the least unique in my absurdity.

## How is the point tipping?

I think it is entirely in my own psyche. I see no sign of a

general recognition that Pi is so insanely aggrandised nor any diminution in the expression of it throughout the population of this land. So it is me that is tipped. I am the point here, an irony, as it could easily be another aspect of my Pi as I secretly perceive it. Thinking about the Ivory Tower mentality at six this morning, I fell into deep sleep again and had a sequence of short dreams that showed my absurdity. As I woke up, thinking that the day was another nightmare to be lived through, I remembered an essential point not yet fully tipped. This is the Area of the Insult. I remembered myself as a small boy with a glass pea-shooter (an aptly self-dangerous weapon) and how I would hide in long grass and pepper passers-by with unripe hawthorn berries. At that time, appropriately, I first heard the aphorism: 'Sticks and stones may break my bones, but names will never hurt me'. I didn't believe it then, nor for seventy years afterwards. But now I do. A year or two ago, I was having an argument with a friend in which I was attacking belief-icons. My interlocutor became irritated with me and my persistence (and my loftiness in my Ivory Tower, presumably) because she started name-calling. The critical phrase was that I am a 'bolshie old geezer'. I was cut to the quick. I could never forgive her. I have only just forgiven her. What I had told myself was that she had offended a fundamental principle of civilisation, she had moved from the object to the subject, attacking me rather than the question being discussed. Bullshit! I was just angry at being criticised. I cannot bear to be criticised. I hate being praised, too, if I get a whiff of condescension. In other words, my Pi is mountainous.

## The Pi Burden

It is also an absurd burden. Being personally important may be bred in the bone, enshrined in the genes, the stuff of survival, and so on, but does it have to weigh so heavily? How far can Pi be diminished? People struggle for humility, believing it to be a good thing. But humility is just the other side of the importance coinage. The female head of the monstrous House of Windsor pronounced herself as 'humbled' by the massive junketing of her Jubilee. What nonsense she speaks. Humbled by adulation? Since when? She was just swanking, as all megalomaniacs do. To be seriously less Pi is actually a massive shift of consciousness. A very tricky shift, too. If I get caught up in the massiveness of my effort I will start congratulating myself on the effort or the achievement and the snotty little ego will have won again. How, then, can it be done? Where is the tipping? It lies somewhere in the territory of, 'I can't be bothered with it.' Yes, a deep exasperation. A flood of nausea gushing through the psychic catacombs. 'To hell with it!' rings around the space in one's soul. Maybe, even, a large dollop of, 'I won't!' The golden glow of self-disgust shines upon the scene. 'Not on your nelly!' I say.

## The Fabulous Four

Thinking on, there arise the Fabulous Four qualities of my kind of Pi: without doubting their merit I was always in thrall to Teaching, Preaching, Leading and Reforming. However lustful, petty, irritable, or greedy I might be 'on the surface', deeper down I was, more or less unknowingly, in the grip of more powerful motives. The teaching impulse involved egoic superiority, a need to dominate, a wish to spread myself everywhere. Preaching, though atheistic, was spiritual in the sense of operating from a transcendent position. As for leading, I was committed to the centre stage and the need to make others do the 'right thing'. Reforming was based on criticism of others (and myself, to be fair) and the wish to improve existence. I had plenty of models for this behavioural syndrome. Epicurus, Abraham, Jesus, Buddha, umpteen saints and gurus, gods, God, doctors, judges, schoolmasters, policemen, parents, and even everyday friends and colleagues, were all at it, teaching, preaching, leading and reforming like billy-ho.

**Free-Fall**

It is fair to acknowledge the widespread employment of these methods, but it does not redeem me, nor others. For me, these behaviours are destructive. I think, as it happens, they have mixed results for everyone, both practitioners and receivers, but that is another tipping-point. The fact is that these habits are fading in myself. Even as I write this I cringe at the thought that, by writing my story, I am still indulging in the Fabulous Four. But at least I know it and decry it. The relief of knowing that I do not have to teach, preach, lead, or reform anyone or anything is wonderful, a new freedom. I realise that my Pi will not decline easily, but it is in some kind of free-fall. The important thing is that it is voluntarily falling rather than merely being suppressed. A new state of being is arising spontaneously. It feels as if the Void is enclosing me

without the sense of loss or abandonment that it often induces.
May the point go on tipping.

# Essay 18
# Marcus and Dante in the Inferno

## Man in the Making

Precisely at thirty-five years of age, Marcus had obliged himself with a mid-life crisis. It was the year 1966. He wrote to his mother explaining his terminal distress, making it clear that suicide was on his cards. She didn't answer - at least, not to his cry of despair. There's not much you can say to someone, even a son, who comes to recognise the fatuity of his existence. She was probably wise to leave him in the hands of Ellen - after all, he had chosen her to be his life-partner, not his mother. By the time his mother died of a heart-attack, just three years after his cri de coeur, Marcus had a new career and new enthusiasm for life. But his basic temperament had not altered. If he did not quite descend into the upper reaches of hell again, it was mainly because he had scared himself so badly in 1966, after several similar previous glimpses into the abyss. From then on, he was stoical, trying to be happy despite everything. It was rather a poor substitute for a satisfactory living, but he left himself in no doubt that it was the best he could expect. By average standards he did pretty well. He stayed faithful to Ellen and earned enough money, without any fiddling, to retire before he was sixty. First smoking, then drinking, didn't do much for his health, however, so he ended up in a coronary care unit not long after the critical date of his seventieth birthday. So, with his liver and heart just intact, and Ellen just holding on to her life, he looked deeper into that abyss and, as it has been said to do, the abyss stared back at him. Apart from Ellen, and quite a number of good friends, he was a man without robust inner resources. His atheism, staunch as it was, didn't help much - not that he expected help from it. He accepted that life was meaningless and purposeless, apart from what he created for himself. There was no conceivable cause for complaint - Job was just an idiot and Jesus a mere conjurer. Grieve as he might, and did, life was just there to be lived and death was there to be died. Then something different happened. A change of awareness, apparently, overcame him. It was not an instantaneous enlightenment, but rather a gradual seepage of something into whatever constituted his debatable soul. The 'something' was hard to identify. He tried, but failed, to find an adequate label. He kept thinking about Epicurus, who seemed to have had a similar 'something'. But most of what Epicurus had written was destroyed, so Marcus couldn't go to Epicurus for help. Buddha and Lao Tze were also possibles, but their messages were hard for him to read.

Spinoza thrilled him but somehow failed to set him fully alight. Marcus was left with his abyss, and largely by himself, as he had no head for nostrums.

### First Glimmerings

The most hopeful sign for him was the autonomous perception of negative personal importance (See Essay Seventeen). This had previously been in an internal box labelled 'low self-esteem' and therefore unrecognised for what it actually was. Similarly, his close attention to Eschenbach's 'Parzival' and to Robert Bly's 'Iron John', were hidden symptoms of a super-serious taking of himself, i.e. excessive personal importance. He had lived for twenty years in a milieu that treated personal 'being' as vastly significant, in contrast to his previous thirty years in science and business, a world in which personal being had been virtually ignored. His painting and writing had been his attempt, then, to have some personal 'being', perhaps 'soul', which became almost a compulsory activity once he had joined in the 'awareness world'. The exposure of Pi was therefore explosively significant for Marcus as an old man. In general, he was suddenly left with 'nothing'. This had also been foreshadowed, had he fully realised it, by other experiences which he had collected in a mind-file entitled 'The Void'.

## Emptiness

Of course he had digested the messages of Zen and Tao. Of course he knew that the Void or the Emptiness were real, and that their realness held the possibility of humankind coming awake and stopping its madness. Of course he knew that god-based philosophies were nonsense. Of course he knew that the rape of the planet had to cease or we'd all be ditched. All this knowledge and work had entered into his tiny consciousness. Yet he was still as much a Big Bad Wolf as the next man, or woman. One of his best experiences, apart from the sheer beauty of the near-death crisis in his coronaries, was in a meditation in a house in the town of Knaresborough. He had been asked, with the others there, to imagine he was in a crowded room looking for an exit door. He found the door and exited. He entered a long tunnel, as one often does in exit meditations, and wandered down an endless darkness until his path was barred by an opaque veil of tough material similar to polythene. His internal messenger told him he was facing the Void. In all previous such encounters he had respectfully withdrawn, on the assumption that when one meets the Void it was the definitive experience in itself and should be left intact. He could not have explained why. Nor could he say why, on this occasion, he burst through the veil so as to enter the Void. Inside there was apparently infinite space occupied by an infinity of tiny particles. Well, he had previously had a similar experience without having to penetrate a veil. He had attributed that to an encounter with the 'great continuity' in which everything that ever was or will be is contained. So he had been an observer of the 'great continuity'. He often referred to this infinite matrix. The absurdity of his position had never occurred to him. Nor did it in Knaresborough. He was charmed, as were his companions, by this encounter with the 'absolute', as if he had been introduced to God and shaken the gigantic paw. Now, this preposterous assumption came back to taunt him, a revelation unconnected with the fact that he was an atheist anyway. As with Pi, how could he suppose that he had *observed* the infinite? He had failed to recognise the epitome of human hubris. He had, of course, envisioned himself as separate from the infinite mass of particles. Just as a professor of astrophysics might carelessly mistake himself as an authority of some obscure kind, watching from afar, judging and appraising what was apparently 'out there'. What Marcus almost began to suspect, though it was still early days in his late journey, that *he was only one of the infinity of particles.* Of course he would have known that all along, as we all do. Allegedly. But *feeling* his infinitesimal importance was a different matter. For a dramatic exposure of the imbecility of Pi, you can't beat this, unless you go back to mediaeval time and meet Dante Alighieri, for whom Pi was a cosmic journey.

## The Divine Comedy

Of the many characterisations of a fantasy afterlife, in this case a long residence in hell, there are few that excel the severity and elaborateness of Dante's psychopathological wandering. Marcus must have dreamed one night that he was Dante, because he felt an urge to know him better. Maybe he had been waiting for him. He approached Dante's poetry with little enthusiasm but was intrigued by the idea of an infantile anima, who sent to Dante a companion in the form of Virgil, and most of all a grand tour of a gigantic and intricately constructed city of torture. Marcus had been unaware, before, that mediaeval Catholicism seemed to gain enormous pleasure and satisfaction from a real or imagined nightmare, a revelry that lingered on after the Reformation in the vicious foretelling of Calvin and Luther. In other words, religion per se likes to drag itself through blood and ordure, and thereby praise its own purity. What Marcus had not expected was that Dante was a megalomaniac and lived in a culture of megalomania. Marcus was no historian. He didn't even believe in history. He regarded it as a 'bunch of dubious stories', but the truth of Dante's self-adoration was incontestable from the mad posturing in the poetry. So this was a central story of Western death and romance and spirituality? Marcus noted that, if nothing else, poetry had the merit of showing a society's well-hidden arse.

### Beatrice the Golden Girl

She had the sense to die young. For a mere twenty-four summers she had graced the city. Dante had seen her from a distance, now and then. Enough, it seems, to fix her absolutely in his psyche as the personification of some holy virgin or other. There is no way of knowing anything useful about her. She was just a cipher. What a life! Yet there was a life. Not as Dante would have seen it, though he could presumably have seen it in such a small town. The whole 'muse' story seemed to Marcus to be a piece of meretricious romanticism not to say sentimentality. Beatrice married a banker, Simone dei Bardi in 1287, it seems, a marriage that was brief because Beatrice died in 1290. Dante, the allegedly besotted gazer from afar (briefly meeting her on only two occasions, first when he and she were about 8 or 9 years old, and nine years later, in 1283, for a moment by the Arno river), also married (Gemma Donati) in 1285 and had children with her. His entrancement by Beatrice did not, apparently, preclude him from erotic congress with an ordinary mortal. None of this would matter more than one of the fatuous encounters in a modern soap were it not for the mountainous spiritual erection based on this fragile patch of ground. The Catholic Church more or less hallowed the whole nonsense, as it would, and 'hell' received an elaborate and splendid PR endorsement. The significance of all this resonates strongly with Marcus as he realises how he and his contemporaries are still being mind-raped by those old devils in surplices and jewels who ruled us all by harping on our guilt and our sin. The 'dirty old men and the virginal girl' is an old, old, criminal fantasy. Dante was a clean young lad who could be presented as a genius of language and a clear-eyed observer of human woe, backed up by this witless, idealised, female. The whole drama is sick and repellent, yet it is purported to embody the essence of spiritual love and the dangers of fleshly indulgence. It is even said that Dante, and his talented predecessor and 'guide', Guido Cavalcanti, virtually invented lyric poetry. Marcus tried to read Dante and expressed a preference for Dylan Thomas and the old curmudgeon, Larkin, lyrically valid for him, at least.

## Beatrice the Muse

Beatrice, safely dead, could blossom into a divine authority, not unlike the spurious gravitas of Jesus's god-mother-surrogate. She, in Dante's hot brain, was responsible for appointing Virgil, no less, as his guide through hell. For Marcus, this alone would have been enough to bring Dante's massive egomania into the open. A nice touch, too, speaking sarcastically, was the displacement of Virgil, a mere pagan, by the sweet Catholic maiden, Beatrice herself, for the closing scenes of the great sin-tour ending up in 'Paradiso' and the last cantos of 'Purgatorio'. Another hilarious touch was the reservation of the best seats in hell for the poets, poncing about in the first circle. It seemed that Dante was actually in a psychic inferno of his own, a clinical depression indeed, in the early 1300's and the 'Divina Commedia' was what emerged from his twenty-year self-exile in madness. He escaped life in 1321 without clarifying which circle of hell he intended to inhabit. In this tragi-comedy of paranoia and remembered lust for the unavailable, Dante imagines Beatrice as his living dead consort. An actual woman would have limitations, obviously, as Marcus was only too well aware, but a mind-girlie was something else. Here was hell ennobled and rather enjoyable to the didactic observer, accompanied by the great dead poet, Virgil, and the sublime all-wise beauty, Beatrice. Dante was not so mad that he didn't know how to coddle himself egoically.

### The Danger for a Modern Man

Marcus lacked Dante's resources yet suffered Dante-like tortures. He epiphanied. The virtue of religious addiction became clear to him at last. As a rational man, Marcus had no hell to keep him warm. His freedom from god-delusions was a savage one. He knew that he was unimportant. Whereas a god-believer convinced himself of his importance. Marcus knew he had no significance beyond his tiny circle of friends. He was a number; a mere statistic. His mystical experiences were many and lovely, but it was not obvious that they had any significance beyond his little existence and his huge imagination. Hell, on the other hand, like heaven, gave a person meaning, even a purpose. If you were convinced that death was a door to another dimension, rather than mere oblivion, then you need not despair. Your ego was guaranteed a square meal for eternity. For Marcus, the prospect of atheistic death was far from unpleasant - after all, there were many hellish features of life and not a lot of heaven, especially as age and infirmity tightened their merciless neckhold. He might suffer the despair of irrelevance but was at least spared the terror of a lived-in abyss beyond the last breath. Marcus's main problem was his lack of control over his own existence. His death seemed to be the business of thousands of busybodies. He couldn't die when and how he wanted to do it. He observed Dante's world-view with derisive horror. The litany of tortures in the hell city was both risible and obscene. It was as if the authors of the fantasy had taken the lowlife reality and stretched and expanded it into a comprehensive world of nauseating misery. And it seemed that paradise was rather iffy as well. A masterpiece of religious lunacy, then. The whole thing. It's one virtue, if that's the right word, was that it made the mediaeval mind swell with its own importance, however revolting the prospect.

### Has Hell Died?

No. It has merely shifted its psychic dimensions. Marcus, like any other modern Englishman, did have a moral sense and an aptitude for guilt. Whether these mental knee-jerks were inherent, congenital, learned, or somehow implicit in conscious existence, the fact was that Marcus was as troubled in his mind as any mediaeval peasant. Not necessarily in his aware, educated, intelligent mind, but more likely in the underpinnings, the so-called unconscious or semi-conscious, whatever they might, or might not, be. He was also all his ancestors rolled into one mucky ball. Yet, being intellectually free at last, he had no personal significance or great inherent worthiness to offset the horrors. He had thrown out the bathwater and held on to the smelly, stupid, noisy, baby. So this was Marcus's inferno, with no Beatrice or Virgil to see him through. How could a 21st Century Englishman, beneficiary of the Enlightenment, free from the stultifying absurdities of religion and suspicious of the self-satisfied gurus of science, how could such a man have an ounce of self-regard? How could he not shake with fear at the prospect of a hospice-death? And how could he find the energy and strength to stand it when he knew it was all for absolutely nothing? This is another hell. A bigger and better hell, perhaps. Marcus could strive to be good, honest and caring, but there were no hell-pains to be eased by this effort. Being a good man was a gratuitous act. He might argue that virtue was its own reward, but how could it be? How could there be any reward at all? Marcus might take self-satisfaction to the cremation oven, but so what? At one time, when he was younger, Marcus was persuaded by the argument that love had to be unconditional to be worth its full value. When this bit of unctuous sophistry was exposed for the fraud it was, Marcus grieved for the lost concept. Now it was the same with virtue. Like love, it was all too obvious that virtue must be unconditional, otherwise it would not be virtue. He couldn't say to his beloved, 'Ellen, I will love you unconditionally if you will do the same for me'. Nor could he cry out to the unheeding universe, 'I will be unconditionally virtuous so long as you make it worth my while'. Well, he could, if he was prepared to see himself as a fool, for that was the meretricious bargain that Catholicism had always sought from its godhead.

## What, Then?

Now he had lost everything how could Marcus live a worthwhile existence. The obvious answer - that he would just have to - was nonsensical. To live a good life because there was nothing of value in your life was not an obvious formula for a Western man, great as it might be for a Bhudda. To his credit, Marcus did look along that path and took hesitant steps along it. He sensed a sense in it, somewhere. He had at least come to the realisation that it was hell that caused his problems, or at least his failure to stare his hell in its ugly face. The strongest card up Marcus's sleeve was the one he had always denied. He had a volatile temper. It scared him. He avoided it. He suppressed it. It made him feel 'hellishly guilty'. How could he know it was his primary saving grace? He was perceived by his friendlier friends as a brilliantly civilised, urbane, sensitive man with, periodically, the burning rage of a samurai. (Or was that how he perceived how his friends perceived him?) He could irritate, too, by his refusal to let an argument slip away into the long grass. He would go on fighting long after others had grown bored or resigned. This hotness of temperament bothered him intensely, yet he could do little to diminish it. It was his inability to mediate himself that bothered him and it was this that brought him salvation. It was, significantly, also his temperamental passion for truth, particularly an angry reaction to what he saw as self-serving falsehood or impossible certainty, that powered his apparent irritability. Beyond everything else, he was contemptuous of what he saw as his own infantilism, his easily stimulated fear and remorse, and his anxiety about how others felt about him.

### In The Blood

All these features combined to make what he suffered as his own character. They constituted his hell and paradise. He had always failed, until now, to see the value of his bundle of temperaments. As his imaginary, and maybe actual, social milieu would expect, he had been apologetic rather than triumphant. But now that he faced the emptiness outside and within, the abyss, the non-meaning of the universe and himself in it, he had the revelation that it was the bundle of temperaments that *were* the meaning of his life. As a lapsed Christian, an atheist from toddlerdom onwards, he had had the typical mindset despite knowing better. That mindset was embodied in the phrase, 'There must be more to life than this', the aphorism that ruled life in the Western 'civilisation'. In this inanity dwelt the idea of deity, so that the unbeliever, Marcus, merely suffered psychic amputation. He had received, or dealt himself, a dud hand. He had missed the whole point, which was that he himself was the point of himself.

### Inherence

The bundle of temperaments actually *were* his significance. He didn't need 'meaning', 'purpose', and especially not 'eternity', because he was his own universe, God, or validation. He couldn't help it. He might curse and growl sometimes, but that was just who and what he ineluctably was. His drives were beyond mind or purpose, they were his drives and they made him whether he liked it or not. Like a wild animal in the forest he just *lived* his meaning and would die when he had finished with it or it had finished with him. There was not more to life than this. Nor needed to be.

### Early Morning Light

Marcus was suffering the dawn blues, that time when the bodymind is still half asleep and desires elbow sense aside. Despite all his wise thinking, he still longed for that elusive conviction that all was actually very well in his world. He knew it was and he knew it wasn't, his mindset was now suffused with agnosticism, he was an open book in which he hesitated to write anything at all. He thought about his situation sympathetically. While he was not sorry for himself he felt a soft sadness for the pain and panic of his existence. Paradoxically, he also felt grief at the knowledge that, unlike diamonds, he was not forever. It should have been a consolation for him, being certain he approached complete oblivion. But there was a problem. Although he knew well enough that there was no more to life that just living it, and dying it when the time came, there was the nagging difficulty of the soul, that conundrum that always bobbed up and down when he thought he had reached a stoical resolution. He had recently written, much to his surprise as a loyal atheist, that when everything had been burnt away in the incinerator - or consumed by the hordes of saphrophytic small janitors - there might remain an insubstantial, a non-substantial, essence of his being. He used the word 'soul' to label this airy remnant, in the same way as he might think of spoken words or feelings of love as having no substance yet somehow moving into the atmosphere and still being part of the living world. This was not so much a belief, or a surmise, as a small article of faith that the world was not so arrantly wasteful that it would throw away the best parts of a dying being. There was no sense in this, he knew. No scientific sense, at least; and religion didn't 'do' sense. Marcus had heard all the stories about post-mortem 'survival' and regarded them as lunacy. So why was there this odd feeling that a non-material soul was lurking inside him waiting to be released into a specialised realm inaccessible to crass physicality? It both bothered him and consoled him. Which was another puzzle: why should he be interested in something outside his mindset. Did it mean, treasured thought, that his mind-set was incomplete, or flawed, or just wrong? He could live with science being error-prone, and religion being insane, but could he live with the possibility that his scepticism was also invalid? Was 'sense' merely a moving target?

### Another False God?

Marcus did worship something: it was called **'truth'**. A strange predilection, because he knew perfectly well that 'truth' could not survive scrutiny. At best, he might excuse himself for loving the *idea* of truth. He might also live it to the extent that he always pursued it zealously, as he would a probably-extinct creature. The problem with science was, for

Marcus, that its truth was always relative, subject to degree or error, while the truth of religion was always and merely a mad fantasy. Why, therefore, assume that his idea of total annihilation was the right, i.e. the truthful, interpretation of physical death? How would he know? How could he know, when he knew nothing else for sure. How could he know something so important when he knew that all science and religion, i.e. all knowledge in effect, was probably bosh? Marcus could 'see' his deceased mother and father and his dead sisters and he dutifully attributed this vision to a safely unknowable function called 'memory'. The people themselves were long dead and therefore non-existent. But their souls were: where? Was he sure that their souls were nowhere? No souls at all? How could he know such a thing? Did he know such a thing? Or was it just a scientific probability? Another thing: while he was pretty sure he didn't have a permanent, solid, Marcusian self but, if anything, a moving bit of a Buddhist sea, he was less sure that he hadn't a unique essence, a primary beingness inherited at conception or birth. If he felt anything in this area it was essence rather than self while ego was a preposterous shadow on the wall of his internal world and best ignored or shot. Was there any particle of truth in this apparent arrangement? He thought about his adored Balinese cat, now dead, and could not be sure that the creature's soul was not sitting beside him, in some formless form, when he read the newspaper and ate his breakfast. He *felt* the cat's presence and enjoyed the 'illusion'. The cat and he had a shared soul-insubstance. Nonsense, sure, but what was sense? What did he know, for NonGod's sake?

## Another Way of Seeing It

He had made a rod for his own back, sure enough. The rod was concreted rationality, as bad as any fossil creed or science credo. Why did he cling on to this tarbrush of certainty having thrown all the other pitch away? Did he, perhaps, imagine that he was somehow carrying the grail of truth in his backpack? It was all very well to call up the ghost of Occam to drive off the swarm of believers, but wasn't he also merely a blind believer? It was, he began to realise, all a matter of emotion. Perverse and inconsistent emotion, at that. He was beating his back with the lash of logic, a fantasy of truth that he had allowed to set in his mind - even begged it to ossify there. Why had he done this? Well, why does anybody believe anything? In this context, his mulishness was maybe forgivable. He had seen living things die and rot or burn away. The evidence of his senses was irrefutable. Dead things were fundamentally different from alive things, it was there to see in front of his eyes. Besides, he had been indoctrinated with the biochemistry of it. He knew the formulae and equations. Death was definitely death, a one-way reaction, perfect entropy. Yet there was the unanswerable problem of soul, or less poetic, the riddle of consciousness. It wasn't in the formulae and the equations. Dissection of the brain and spinal column failed to disclose a substance or tissue that could be identified as consciousness. Anatomically it did not exist. But functionally it was everywhere. Was it legitimate, therefore, to have any ideas about existence when the basic process remained undisclosed? Admittedly, materialistic brain scientists might say that consciousness was a product of neural activity. The brain, they said, made consciousness like the bone marrow made blood corpuscles. No mystery there, then? Obviously, by this simple theory, death was the cessation of consciousness-production when the brain stopped making it, being itself kaput. Marcus wrote poetry. It was his way of bypassing boredom and chaos, his normal perceptions. He was challenged to write verse about the five senses. This was the beginning of his poem:

### Aristotle's Little Dragons, The Famous Five.
Here there be dragons of multiple meanings.
In this vast sea of consciousness they do breed.
At first there were only five, Aristotle's children:
Dragons of his mighty mind. A mind, supreme
In opinion of itself, with a quintet of scaly senses.
They saw, they heard, they felt, they smelt, they tasted,
And thus he conquered for two thousand years and more.
While consciousness drags its feet, an endless mystery.
But yet, imagine a mind without the senses, as blank
As a lifeless sea, or a laptop lacking a whiff of software.
Could consciousness exist without a jot of input data?
Is there an overwhelming question going begging?
Does mind actually exist except in our imagination?
We either downgrade thinking or upgrade sensing:
We can't have our consciousness-cake and eat it.
There's more. It's time to catch the bus of neuroscience.

That bus trundles down the dilapidated road of logical positivism. In writing the poem he retraced his biological learning to see how the idea of five senses fitted reality as it now appeared to scholars in this field. What he discovered astonished him even though he suspected that his received information may have aged as much as he had. He found that the entire body is a matrix of sensory centres. It was indeed hard to see how the whole body was other than conscious, in that it seemed to be a massive brain, or a massive consciousness. It was as if consciousness hadn't been 'discovered, identified and explained' because the whole being actually was consciousness. It could not possibly objectify itself. There was also the question of numbers. It was easy to get lost in the practical illusion of singleness. But a human being was 'made of'' billions and billions of cells of massive diversity and it was colonised be an even larger community of other life-forms. The natural reality was vastly more complex than everyman's simple idea of biological or medical reality. Marcus had dabbled in several realities during his life and 'nature' had always transfixed him. It was nature, glorious, beautiful, dangerous, foul, and cruel nature, that excited him, made him feel alive, mediated complexes and guilts. He had become a Druid at one stage, a three year 'degree' matching his BSc. Looking at the 'senses' poem he had an urge to write a Druidic counterbalance:

### THE GROVE

Now I have it, now I don't, now I do again.

Again that place of all places for the sacred and the sane.

Before the multiple invasions, pagan ancient ones

Made this land and worshipped blood-stained suns.

One thing stands supreme, the survivor of the years,
The place within the human soul that holds all of our tears.
Wild places call to me, gardens hold me in a soft embrace,
Even an enthusiastic allotment puts a smile upon my face.
But there's a place deep in my mind ready to remember
The mystery of trees, presences in summer or December.
There, at last, I made my grove, a temple of the mind
A place inside me where I could sing, and weep, and find
Unique reality of being, leaving fatuous doctrines behind.
I walk through flowery pastures, by hedgerows and streams,
Until I reach the grove and enter as if walking into dreams.
Trees surround me in a circle like contemplating towers.
I walk towards the centre, the circle widens and the hours
Coalesce into a single moment wherein time's stillness I swim
In an expanding lake, around an island, letting life and limb
Carry me to the essence of my being: flower, fruit, and seed
I stand within the tree of life growing on the island and feed
On water, light and air. I am the other form of life, a creator
And when I return to my old self I am acting in a theatre.
I have to leave here, for now, and go back to my no-place
Where I will talk and think and work and look from face to face,
In the modern world, but not of it, the grove is where I live,
A garden wilderness where I have nothing but everything to give.

## Fruit and Seed

Marcus saw a synergy between the two poems, bringing him new comprehension. First, he reviewed the history of himself and was awe-struck by the magic of it, for instance the forgotten fact that he had begun as a single cell with a diameter of a tenth of a millimetre. He had never thought in this way before. When faced with death or failure he had overlooked his extraordinary origin, which made him realise that instead of shock at the end of things he ought to celebrate that he had come so far. More than this, there was the thought that nothing was guaranteed in the rush of life, all life, on the planet. And every living thing was obliged to run a gauntlet that started with a microscopic speck. He was the seed inside the fruit on the tree on the island in the lake in his Grove.

So what about the soul? Was it in that microscopic single cell? Or was it everywhere and in everything? Did the Great Continuity imply a permanent omnipresent soul? Was the vaunted human soul merely a hyperbole for the vast diffuse soul of nature itself? Did he, as part of the universal soul, need to see himself in the proper context and drop the egotism of individuality? If so, how? Maybe no need to try? Let it be? Then the next and perhaps final shock: could everything, including 'soul', be merely by-products of the faulty machinery of the human psyche? All very well to dwell on ideas such as universal consciousness, soul, 'God' or Great Continuity, but all of these were just emanations from the heat of the human mind and of no other value or significance. Nor need they be. Even the fear, panic, pain, grief, of humanness were all mere afflatus, undivine, unremarkable, and as casual and inevitable as love or beauty; all just blades of grass on an endless plain. And these very words, the marks being made on the paper, are just specks of ink. If there were to be any reality beyond human imaginings, we wouldn't, couldn't, know. It was a relief for Marcus, as it is for this moving pen, that he

MINDWALKS BY MICHAEL SCOTT

didn't necessarily have to worry about soul or anything else because it was all imagination, just steam blowing out of his head. The deepest possible level of non-importance of his person was a place of perfect rest. This was the place he sought. Absolute safety. Absolute unimportance of himself. He could live happy. He could die happy. All was well in a state of absolute ignorance and absolute insignificance. End of story.

## Essay 19
## An Epicurean Journey

### The Logical problem of evil

A formulation of the problem of evil often attributed to Epicurus:

*1. If an all-powerful and perfectly good god exists, then evil does not.*

*2. There is evil in the world.*

*3. Therefore, an all-powerful and perfectly good god does not exist.*

### Benedict and Delia

As far as I know, this modern pair were never lovers, though you can't be sure of that in a context which embodies an updated version of the New-Age enterprise, which is how I encountered them. I have evoked the memory of the great ancient Greek philosopher Epicurus for the purpose of studying these two extraordinary people who, had they lived in Greece 2,400 years ago, would, or should, have been part of his Epicurean school. A few words on Epicurus, to establish that context. Two key words for him are *aponia,* absence of pain, and *ataraxia,* peace and freedom from fear. He followed these ideals, as best he could, and devoted himself to a self-sufficient life surrounded by beloved friends. He did not deny that gods might exist but refused to recognise them as having any relevance for humankind. Epicurus was an atomic materialist. His materialism led him to a general attack on superstition and divine intervention. He believed that pleasure is the greatest good. But the way to attain pleasure was to live modestly and to gain knowledge of the workings of the world and the limits of one's desires. The new religious establishment of Constantinian Christianism obliterated most of Epicurus's work during the decades after his death but his legacy survives, if only in the misleading term 'epicurean', meaning, now, luxury and discerning taste.

## Enneagram Seven

Sometime in the relatively recent past a system of human personality typing was discovered that incorporates some Epicurean concepts. One of the nine personality types identified in the Enneagram system, Number Seven, is usually called the Epicure. This is a typical summary of the Enneagram Seven personality: Sevens are outgoing, positive, multi-talented, and high-spirited. On the low side, they can become depressed when frustrated and may also misapply their gifts. Alternatively, they can become manically busy and unintegrated. They are easily drawn into new and enticing activities but can run out of energy or be undermined by their own impatience or even annoyed by their self-inflicted, recurrent, storms of enthusiasm. When life is going well and they are concentrating on worthwhile goals, Sevens are likely to appear joyful and fulfilled. They are especially afraid of deprivation and pain, yet may risk considerable danger for the sake of new experiences or to fulfil their pressing needs. The Enneagram Seven yearns strongly for freedom and happiness, for worthwhile experiences to maintain the momentum of excitement, and loves to be busy to avoid boredom or sublimate distress. With friends and lovers, Sevens tend to waspishness under duress and can be dismissive when disappointed. Otherwise, they may be extravagantly loving and concerned in an expansive mood.

### Benedict and Delia as Epicureans

It is not easy to type people according to any system that is not banal and obvious. In fact, the process of Enneagram typing is a major psychological, spiritual and emotional process. Getting the corrrect identification is less important than the learning involved in attempting it. However, Benedict and Delia do fit the criteria very well. As for myself, Marcus, I must confess to being no Epicurean. Ironically, however, in the way of the Enneagram, my type, Enneagram One, the Reformer, happens to find sanctuary by moving into the number Seven slot. An Enneagram One is rather a miserable Type but may find happiness in the Seven position (as opposed to even worse misery in the Enneagram Four position, the Tragic Romantic). So I understand the Seven quite well perhaps even better than if I actually were a Seven myself.

### Incompleteness

If I say that both Benedict and Delia were existentially incomplete, I am not insulting or criticising them. It is likely that inherent in the Enneagram Seven mindset is a search-and-never-find ambiguity. Whether it is because they have Seven-Typeness, or as a mere coincidence, these two people exemplify great appetites for life, great ambition, massive enthusiasms, qualities of fun and joy, yet they seem to lack a talent for finishing their grand strategy. Perhaps it is not a lack. Perhaps it is just impossible for the great optimism of Sevens to make a safe landing. Or maybe their grand strategy is too loosely defined. Benedict died in his early sixties. Delia still lives, but her life is lower-key than one could have expected. Both stars have declined, one by dying too soon, the other by inexplicably drifting - she is still living busily, but lacks any obvious direction. On the other hand, her love of the natural world (and now her enthusiasm for birds), plus her strong sense of and reverence for the inexplicably numinous, enables her to overcome any disappointment and elevates low spirits. Benedict, while he lived, was buoyed up by human achievement generally, by hope for the future, and by his affection for 'old wisdoms' and his sense of the divine. But exactly how happy he was, I do not know. This is, however, an Enneagram Reformer speaking. It is a partial and biased view, by definition. The answer is to look at the whole picture. Moving beyond the mere question of personality type, which is embedded in a system, it might be more productive to look at the nature of ambition in relation to Benedict, Delia and myself, their friend Marcus.

## Hubris

Although a crime in ancient Greece, hubris is more a psychological state in modern usage. It has even been elevated to a 'syndrome', particularly relating to disordered mentality of people in positions of power. It is a state of arrogance or over-confidence. However, to aim high, to want to achieve something worthwhile, may also be the best part of the human psyche. Benedict and Delia both aimed high from their youth. With little advantage but inborn talent they became local teachers and leaders in the field of human development. Benedict founded a school of human relations, to which Delia found her way while developing her own interests. They also aspired to the 'transpersonal', and worked together in a learning community focusing on spirituality. That was the context in which I met them and shared their interests. Undoubtedly, their work had considerable effect on others. Benedict's writings became significant globally. To the extent that human failure is due to poor education and pedestrian objectives, his efforts did achieve some important whistle-blowing. But Delia failed to gain power in this enterprise and Benedict also at last retreated into a background position. I just retreated into writing and painting, a world of my own. The picture for all three of us was, therefore, a more or less reducing personal importance in the fields of development to which we had aspired.

### Failure

Is it unfair to label this as failure? Did we all fail to 'achieve something worthwhile'? The answer to both questions is 'yes'. To label a 'reduction in personal importance' as failure is to presume that increase in personal importance would have been preferable or superior in the chosen fields. This assumption should be challenged. As to the second question, of course we 'failed to achieve something worthwhile', but was this necessarily undesirable? Referring briefly to the Zen stories of spiritual arrogance resulting in the Void, the issue is whether we are right to set ourselves elevated targets with the assumption that we are specially chosen or qualified to change the nature of the wild bull, trapping it, taming it, bringing it in our own domestic circle. In the ox-herding stories of Zen, the 'pilgrim' becomes a post-void vagabond, which begs the whole question of what we are trying to do with our lives. It follows that Benedict, Delia and Marcus were presuming to have a job to do in the world, a job-temporal or a job-spiritual, but a job in either sense involving changing the world (and themselves in it). People like us say, 'I want to make a difference', as if the wish validated the attempt. It's like wanting to climb Everest or swim the Atlantic and ignoring the question: 'Why?' There are many cases in which the answer that is given is, 'Because it is there' and there is general failure to recognise that this is no answer at all. The issue seems to be, therefore, that much more thought needs to go into the initial assumption, that the goal needs to be clear and untainted by corruption, such as the need for acclaim or fame or self-esteem. Why, otherwise, presume to change others and the world in which they live? How is the mandate created? What is the moral or spiritual purity of the impulse? If the goal passes the tests, it is also important to establish what would be the way of identifying completion of the goal? It might be all very well to travel (and toil) hopefully, but how will we know when we have reached the end of the journey? Or, if we realise we have made a mistake, should we not accept that fact and think again rather than either plodding on without enthusiasm, or giving up and sulking?

## The Wrong Track

I must be careful to avoid the errors I have been lambasting. The three of us, like most go-getters I know, started from the assumption that we had to choose a 'way of success', a path leading to the 'promised land' of our ideals. That is what good human beings try to do. Less good humans choose paths leading to personal gain, fame or power. Even the good ones tend to appreciate some of these by-products too. But Benedict, Delia and I, at least in our mature years, have tried to follow the path of practical goodness. It is probably the wrong track even for the best of us, perhaps especially for the best of us. And it is very hard to say why this could be the case. 'Surely', an interested observer might say, 'Surely it must be right to follow the path of practical goodness?' The answer to that question can only be, 'Yes, if you are absolutely certain of what is practically good. And even that might not be enough if you are hooked into personal satisfaction, in some way associated with what is practically good.'

## Evolution Rewind

I had tried to tell Benedict and Delia why the situation was pretty hopeless. I had said that a path of practical goodness had never led anywhere nor had it reached anywhere, that the world was in an awful mess and getting worse, that good people could not turn the world around even if they were justified in trying to do it. Well, maybe I was just trumpeting my own despair. Perhaps I was not. Yet I had changed myself. I will say that again. I had changed myself. I had rewound the brief tape of my own history, and the almost as brief tape of human history. How brief is that? I ask myself. Divide 200,000 years, the time *Homo sapiens* had been around, by 4,000,000000 years, the (short-scale) time any life has been around, and, if my sums are right, humankind had been on earth one twenty thousandth or less of the time since life was invented. If I take the biblical week as the time of earthly life, humanity had arrived about one minute before midnight on the 7th day. Our wonderful species had hardly drawn breath yet it had almost destroyed the planet already. Mankind is evidently lethal, following its established precepts. Those precepts must be wrong. 'So must mine,' had said I. To be fair to my species, I had then taken into account the inheritance of the carnivores going back to *Tyrannosaurus* seventy million years ago, plenty of time for man to have accumulated genetic bad material, if that theory made sense i.e. if humankind could be exonerated from its failure by its mere genetic lineage. But then, what of the much-vaunted human consciousness, or the fabulous brain? Had it invented the idea of the practical good only to decline into absolute stupidity? So, what was this idea of the practically good? How could it be demonstrated or proved, given the historical reality. Not at all, it seemed. Much better, declared I, to change oneself. Just oneself. Leaving other people alone. Possibly. But where was the general practical goodness in that? Where did such an idea come from? Surely practical goodness must be directed at the entire living world. A salvo of goodness from one's own little boat out across the vast sea?

### Challenging the Blueprint

*The fault, dear Brutus, is not in our stars, but in ourselves.*
It comes back to the central absurdity of personal importance,
a Quixotic entity replete with boundless hubris, fed by endless
egotism. 'I want to change the world' is the cry of an inflated
idiot, as I see it. It is overweening enough to think one can
change merely oneself. Yet it is the only *practical* strategy. I
now remembered a meeting with Benedict nearly thirty years
before, at the beginning of our association. I had asked how I
should embark on a career of healing, the calling I felt I had
suppressed in myself for far too long. Benedict had replied,
'Heal yourself. Then your state of being will heal others'. It
felt like a put-down at the time - and it probably was. But
Benedict then conspicuously failed to take his own advice. He
became a guru, while committing sundry minor crimes of
egotism, during his forties and fifties. Benedict at sixty was
not obviously any more effective in his chosen fields than
when he was thirty-five. Perhaps he was, but I could not
detect it. In reality, I suffered significant pain, even damage,
at the hands of Benedict. Our friendship survived, but only
just. To me it seemed that we were about as bad as each other
in that period. Accounts of the lives of other gurus reinforced
the impression that the desire to do good was no guarantee of
personal good behaviour. Did this matter? Was it the message
that mattered and not the messenger? Slowly, erratically, it
dawned upon me that the messenger was all-important and the
message could only, as Benedict had originally implied, be

effective according to the *behaviour* of the messenger. Looking at the total impact of humankind on planet earth, it can only be concluded that human behaviour is disastrous. Even humankind itself suffers at the hands of humankind. So where is the practical goodness, our practical goodness, manifest in the world. Manifestly it is, in bits, here and there. Not enough. Yet it happens. The blueprint is not absolutely rotten. There is something good in us. It is just not good enough nor powerful enough, which is presumably why people like Benedict and Delia embark upon an improvement campaign. It just doesn't work, unfortunately. I concluded that some kind of surrender of personal hubris was necessary, but I couldn't quite see how or why. Hardly surprising. I was only human.

## What Matters?

The surrender that I dimly perceived came unexpectedly. As an Enneagram Type Reformer, I had always taken it for granted that what mattered here on earth was improvement, generally in terms of less pain, less waste, more beauty and so on. It seemed obvious that the point of existence was to make things better. For a few thousand years this assumption had been built in to the practice of placation or worship of the presumed overall master and architect, from whom everything flowed. Heaven had been invented as a compensation for earthly suffering, a place where things were truly better. Hell was the punishment place for bad people. There was a certain mad sense in this theoretical arrangement. But what if such ideas were nonsense? What if it is all down to us? That is what Epicurus thought. Was he wrong? The story goes that he was dying and in agony from kidney stones, yet he sent a message to a friend to say that he was profoundly happy and that everything was wonderful. For me it began to seem that this was the sense in which nothing actually mattered. Complete surrender to reality could relieve a person of soul-suffering and leave him with just the world-pain (or pleasure) which will eventually cease.

### Epicurus, Benedict, Delia and Me.

Live in it, be it, let it be you. Is this the completion Benedict did not quite find and Delia is still finding? Did Epicurus find it? Am I finding it? What is 'it'? Not an 'it'? Not a thing? A place? A process? A state of being? A question? A speculation: are we people who do not have a centre - or who find that we don't have one when we actually look for it. Do other 'types' live within an identity with a presumed centre, as one might say, 'I am a doctor', 'I am a teacher', or 'I am a Christian'? Does the epicurean/idealist have no such security of inner tenure? Delia *did* have a vocation to travel to somewhere she identified as 'the centre' but I understand that this was partly a sense of selfhood, precarious at best, and that she moved away from the 'centre of the existential labyrinth', to move outwards into the world. We discussed the centre-question, and reached the understanding that neither of us had an experience of a centre, as I suspected. If I am right, Delia and I share a secret vocation, and Benedict was part of it too. I suspect that we are all glorifiers. If so, this is a serious affliction for beings existing in the real world. For myself, I realise that my morbid perfectionism is perfectly balanced by a wild idealism. In that sense, at least, I am bipolar. I know that Delia often wakes up in a suicidal flatness which she quickly converts into joyful activity. That's the sort of thing I do as well. I can't say whether Benedict was the same, but he was usually ebullient within a general air of suspicion, as if he didn't quite trust his glory. He was very intelligent, like Delia, so he shone his probing flashlight on everything. Delia accuses me of having a powerful intellect which I use as a battering ram. That alarms me, as a concept. I see my position as much more defensive than offensive. But the 'probing intellect' factor seems to connect the three of us. Presumably it characterised old Epicurus too. This cast and quality of mind and emotion must involve concern about the state of the world. If we are dedicated to glory, we have to try to find it, encourage it, and denounce counterfeit manifestations of it. In that self-important sense we are a fifth column in a civilisation of mediocrity. In that sense, too, we can never be satisfied with ourselves or our lives. We may glory in life but we detest its limitations. If these limitations are built into the basic fabric of existence, as I suspect they are, then we are bound for terminal disappointment.

**The Olympian Spirit**

Ironically, the recent explosion of physical competitiveness (the London Olympics) has made Delia and me seasick. This nationalistic fever is precisely the counterfeit glory we most detest. We have both found ourselves caught in breathless admiration of the strength and grace of exceptional fellow humans, yet we know it is all meretricious. Indeed, the lie at the heart of the Olympics is the same lie that Delia, Benedict and I have been wrestling with for most of our lives. And it is the lie that ultimately exhausts us. It is probably what killed Benedict and is currently confining Delia. I have a daily tussle with it. What is this Olympic-sized lie? I think it is the widespread assumption by mankind that we are the masterpiece of nature. Or at least the most important species. I am not suggesting that Delia wakes up every morning and declares, 'People are just not worth that much, why do they presume so?', though she might. Neither do I. But I could, if I allowed myself. The reality is deeper, anyway, than this thought. It is more a question of how people get to think that humankind is somehow basically meaningful or that it has any conceivable purpose. I mean, of course, a *given* purpose or meaning, as we surely have to create them ourselves for life to be liveable. And, generally, we don't, as a species, do that very well. Hence the reforming zeal of the epicurean/perfectionist. Especially if we do not believe in gods.

## Essay 20
## The Infinite Mountain: A One-Act Play

### The Characters

**Doubting Tom**: Spiritual Rationalism is the buzz: satisfyingly rebellious. But the question is whether I can rationally analyse myself spiritually to find who I am? What am I actually looking for?

**Good Fairy**: I find plurality no challenge at all. I love diversity and a lot of freedom. And the joys of music, nature, and our creative heritage, all sustain me.

**Careful Pilgrim**: I am serene in my being. But freedom has to be tended with great care, with turning to 'the other' in every situation. My stand-by is our history: in our tradition lies our ultimate strength.

**Resolute Gnostic**: I shall never know all the answers so I must keep asking the questions. More and more questions until the answers will become a mountain. I must keep open house on the mountain so that others know they are welcome.

**Mystic Wanderer**: My visions keep me well-informed. On any day I may become powerful in my intuitions or strong from my dreams. Peace is there for me. But the person who finds it necessary to be offensive makes me sad.

**Leading Lady**: My mission is to do good in the world, to keep my personal integrity, and to nurture my family. I have a strong affinity with the Tao and an evolutionary approach to reincarnation.

**Eternal Crone**: I have seen it all and I am not terribly impressed. I want to go on living and not suffer too much, but

I am tired of cant and empty philosophising. Just living with my age and weakness takes all my energy now.

## The Play

Backdrop: a huge window with a view of a white mountain that seems to stretch infinitely upwards and sideways. The room inside is painted white and all the furniture is white. The characters all dress in white. The lights change colour through the spectrum, slowly and gently, so the whole set varies from pure white through to deep indigo. The mountain is always white. The play opens with all seven characters standing at the window looking out at the mountain. A single light from the left side of the stage shows the characters and furniture by means of narrow shadows. From the rear view the characters are identically dressed in white cloaks with cowls over their heads. But each has an identification symbol, the first letter of the second part of their name, i.e. T(Tom), F(Fairy), P(Pilgrim), G(Gnostic), W(Wanderer), L(Lady) and C(Crone). The letters are elaborately shaped and coloured gold. The central figure, G, Resolute Gnostic, turns to face the audience. He throws off his cloak and reveals a jester's costume underneath. He seems sad rather than comical, a tragic, philosophical, fool rather than a lighthearted joker. He declaims loudly but his speech is faulty, he stammers, coughs, cries with pain, laughs hysterically. The letters RG are emblazoned on the front of his tunic. He carries a swagger stick with which he attempts to conduct his own performance. This is his approximate speech:

**Resolute Gnostic:**

'I am. What I am. That am I. Aaaaagh! Ooooohaha! How true, hoo, hoo! Oooo! My pain is exist… isexis… is me as I am. What is this am I am? (Laughs and coughs and retches). I- I- I- I am, am, am, am, a scholar-gipsy… "G- G- G- o- o- o-o-! for they- they- they- call you, shepherd, from the h- h- h-hill…" How long would it take for me to recite all twenty five verses, Eh? Two hundred and fifty lines. A nifty poem by Mat Arnold - he couldn't w-w-w-w-ri-ri-ri-ttt short any more than I can talk l-l-l-l-lonnnnnggggg.'

(Character 'F' turns to face the audience. She is winsome sweet and smiling. As her cloak and cowl drop to the floor her costume is revealed, the sugar plum fairy from a Christmas Tree. She waves a sparkling rod with a terminal star. She speaks with a clear musical voice in a pronounced Geordie accent.)

**Good Fairy:** 'What my friend means to say is that life isn't easy - for most of us perhaps - and we must make the best of it - like Matthew Arnold's nice hero in the poem. You may wish to know that Edmund Blunden said it represents the living ghost in each of us - recollections, wishes, promises - all that sort of thing - not as bad as Jude the Obscure but that was Hardy, wasn't it, a different cup of tea from Arnold - and it wasn't a poem either… the important thing is to keep a proper balance between your "scholar" and your "Gip . .".'

(She is interrupted by character P, who turns to face the audience. He keeps his cloak but the cowl is a mitre seen from the front and the front of his cloak is a coloured ecclesiastical outfit, like a pantomime bishop. He nods and smiles at the first two speakers then launches into what threatens to be a long diatribe about patience or surrender or some such placebo.)

**Careful Pilgrim:** 'Now we need to be careful about Matthew Arnold. I'm not sure that he was one of us. I suspect he may have had a tendency to atheism. Or at least despair. One must be tolerant but also discerning. You also need to be careful about ghosts - except of course the Holy variety (though some of have doubts even about that one). Let's think about this 'scholar-gipsy'. Does he have any true relevance to us? Or is he just a fanciful version of everyman. We all have to settle for what life allows us and it's rather a cowardly thing, perhaps, to go off into a secretive life without a connection to ordinary folk. Now I like poetry, but I want to understand it as well as admire it. I don't understand why my friend Resolute chooses to identify with this scholar-gipsy person. Firstly, he was in a dreadful muddle. Arnold, I mean. The poem is in several disconnected pieces and the end bit about 'Syrtes and soft Sicily' has nothing whatever to do with the first part about shepherds in the fields and neither fits with the stuff about Oxford. Then there's all that business about seeking him here and everywhere like the Scarlet Pimpernel - not to mention the idea of ghostly survival. Does anybody know what he's talking about? Otherwise, can we get on with something useful…?'

'I do', interrupts character T, turning to reveal himself. (He wears jeans and trainers, surmounted by a red shirt, his head shaven, his visage dark and saturnine. But he is smiling, apparently mischievously.)

**Doubting Tom:** 'The Scholar-gipsy is us, each of us and all of us. Don't you get it? Arnold was confused and pretty desperate. His world had fallen apart. 'Dover Beach' is shorter and more to the point. The original story was by Joseph Glanvill, in the 17th century. He was a Latitudinarian and the spirit of Arnold's poem is still latitudinarian two centuries on. The trouble with lack of dogmatism, however, is that nobody knows anything for certain. So Arnold was a free spirit in search of a rock to attach himself too, hence the scholar-gipsy metaphor ...'

He is interrupted, in turn, by a shriek from character L. (She is a slim, middle-aged woman wearing very large spectacles and a distraught expression. She wears a beret and her costume resembles a Parisian bohemian outfit. She could be a painter or a writer. Even an actress.)

**Leading Lady:** 'I'm sick of this and I've never heard of effing Latitudinarians. Come on Tom, what the hell are you talking about.'

**Doubting Tom:** 'I thought someone might ask so I looked them up. I thought it might be another name for the Unitarians, but it's not quite the same thing. The Unitarians don't like the trinity, preferring God to be single, and make a big thing of tolerance, whereas the Latitudinarians were probably even more radical, for example (taking a piece of paper out of his pocket), I quote: *'a group of Anglican Christians active from the 17th through the 19th century who were opposed to dogmatic positions of the Church of England and allowed reason to inform theological interpretation and judgment.'* That's pretty dangerous, you know. Real tolerance and reason aren't liked in religious circles. The natives get restless.'

**Leading Lady:** 'Are you kidding? Are you saying that we are religious anarchists and that is why we are arguing? And a bit fed up? And pretty useless? Do you blame religion for everything?'

(Character W spins around, his arms wide and his face beatific. He is the peace-maker. He is dressed in a pink, shiny, tracksuit with LOVE emblazoned on the chest. His voice is deep and vibrant.)

**Mystic Wanderer:** 'This is one of those epiphanic moments.'

**Leading Lady:** 'Like hell it is! I am totally confused. I thought we were going to have a meeting to decide what we were going to do to improve the project and what we've got is the usual hot air and waffle.'

**Doubting Tom:** 'Well, the 'Scholar-Gipsy' has a good lesson for us. We aren't wasting our time. What we have to do is adjust our collective mindset. It doesn't work very well. Poor old Matthew Arnold was struggling with an inoperative mindset. The poem is an epic mindset battle. We can learn from it. If we want to.'

**Mystic Wanderer:** 'That's what I meant about the epiphanic moment. It is a moment of change. Transformation. The multiverse changes through us and the unknown God comes into being through our consciousness. Our mindset, as you call it, Tom, is just the most recent evolutionary position in the great transformation and of course it is time for it to move further on. Hosannah and hurrah!'

**Leading Lady:** 'My mindset is fixed on the job in hand. We've got till teatime to decide how to spend the rest of our lives. Together or separate. That's it.' (There is an explosive noise from character G. He shouts in staccato, his stutter translated into machine-gun fire. Eventually, he speaks.)

**Resolute Gnostic:** 't- t- t- t- e- e- t- t- t- ime. B- b- b- lime e- e- e- itititit will-take-a-lifetime---- to,oo,oo,oo,oo ----- decide-how-to-spend-the-rest-of-our-lives…'

**Careful Pilgrim:** 'My dear Resolute, was that a philosophical point or just your stutter? No, don't answer. We haven't got the time. 'Teatime' isn't really the cut-off point. Our Leading Lady was just being dramatic. (She protests but he continues unperturbed.) But she's got a point. We need to agree what kind of project we are in. I like Tom's point about the Latitudinarians. The trouble with modern freethinkers who try to be spiritual is that they need a dogma to hold them together and a dogma is precisely what they don't have. No, let me finish this point, please. (Good Fairy has tried to get into the discussion and is waving her wand at Careful Pilgrim - she flounces but shuts up.) We have got to invent a dogma which is both harmless and cohesive…'

**Doubting Tom:** 'But the Latitudinarians did have a dogma: God, Jesus, etc. as if they were standard C of E, and it was just their dislike of a fixed structure that irritated them and they also thought reason was a supreme guide. So, in a way, they were on safe ground. The poor Unitarians, on the other hand, don't have much of a dogma, except a fixed determination to be tolerant of all doctrines and non-doctrines. That's a tough furrow to plough. If anything holds them together, otherwise, it's a somewhat tattered acceptance of the God of Moses, of all things. Therefore, we, as spiritual humanists, have even less than the Unitarians: we don't profess tolerance of religious doctrines and we do not believe in any God, tattered or otherwise. Some people say we are completely stuffed.'

**Careful Pilgrim:** 'What does "stuffed" mean?'

**Doubting Tom:** 'Scuppered. Defeated. Failed. Pointless.'

**Mystic Wanderer:** 'But we aren't. We are evolving towards transcendence. We are becoming God by evolutionary spirituality. That is our dogma, surely?'

**Good Fairy:** 'God' meaning a poetic metaphor, presumably? Otherwise, you shouldn't be a Spiritual Humanist. Please tell me that's what you mean.'

(Character C stirs. As she turns slowly and unsteadily to face the audience, there is silence amongst her companion characters, all of whom turn to look at her. She is quite a vision. Short, thin and bent, she holds on to a walking frame that is gold-plated and studded with semi-precious stones. She wears a tiara flashing with the same stones. Her robe is purple and emblazoned with applique esoteric designs. Her face is beautiful and radiant. But she looks angry. She stamps her frame on the floor.)

**Eternal Crone:** 'I don't have the time or the energy for this. Nor the patience. The issue is quite simple. Are we prepared to discover what a spiritual humanist should be and are we prepared to transform ourselves to meet the criteria? Yes or no?'

**Leading Lady:** 'Well said. Very wise. I had almost

forgotten that we'd decided to re-brand ourselves Spiritual Humanists. Now we've got to say what we mean. As I see it, the whole history of our species is marked by a god-complex, which can include atheist or agnostic doubt. That original mistake dogs us all. It hasn't worked. It won't work. It's just the wrong track. We just have to settle for human qualities and get off the god-bandwagon altogether, haven't we?'

**Eternal Crone:** 'Yes, my dear Lady, but we have still got to come to terms with this spirituality question. I will risk it. Why not. I am a crone. I can risk things. So I say the spirituality has nothing to do with gods or religions, unless you force it to, but is aspiration to transcendence, going beyond or above the lowest common denominator of human nature. It's not as in body versus spirit, there's no split, but it is going to the best and highest manifestation of humanness. It's a hard thing to do. The hardest. The best. Who needs the god-nonsense? Let's go for human spirit. The best choice available. And it can be mystical and sacred and moralistic and all the things religions have stolen from us. I trust that you all agree?'

**Careful Pilgrim:** 'Is this what Arnold was after in the scholar-gipsy poem? Because I didn't think much of that. And I don't see how we can justify quite such a break with historical religious thought. I can go so far towards the Crone's position, but I feel that we must hold on to the sense of 'worship' of the natural order and that there is much in the religions we need to take with us into the future. 'Humanist' must not mean 'godless', because 'god' in the most general and personal sense is the mystery and wonder all around us.

'Humanist' should mean that we, as humans, have awareness of the divine unlike other life-forms, we are a spiritual club in a world of animals and plants.'

(Character G, Resolute Gnostic, has become more and more disturbed by Pilgrim's words and he rushes across to Pilgrim, grabs his arm, spins him round, and points to the white mountain on the backdrop. He is trying to speak. Character L, Leading Lady, joins character G and tries to be his interpreter. But finishes up telling her own story and getting periodic nods of agreement from G. They do seem to be saying the same thing.)

**Leading Lady/Resolute Gnostic:** 'No, no, no, no: human supremacy is bollocks! Evolution is a process and we're part of it - just a part, and we may not stay the course, either. Our work, this project, is about making the best of humanity before it's too late; which it nearly is. The scholar-gipsy is already more than a century old, and Glanvill is three times as old as that, and we haven't got any further than they had. Except some of us have chucked religion altogether, praise be. We are now in survival-mode as never before and only our own spirit can save us. Only our own spirit. So Spiritual Humanism is the way out of the impasse we have created. That is our task.'

(Resolute Gnostic hugs and kisses Leading Lady. Eternal Crone nods and smiles. The other four are still and silent. Then character T gets up and joins the trio. He is deep in thought. He is gazing at the Leading Lady as if bewitched.)

**Doubting Tom:** 'I believe you may have it. Yes. It is a survival matter. The infinite mountain, 'God' if you like, doesn't give a toss whether we survive as a species. Only our preposterous ego made us suppose we mattered at all. But it does matter to us, the humans. So we have to grow up very fast and we can't do that without attention to our spiritual potential - 'spiritual' as you have just defined it. I agree with the three of you. What about the others?'

He turns around to look at the remaining three, Good Fairy, Careful Pilgrim and Mystic Wanderer, characters F, P, and W. They get up from their seats and walk towards the front of the stage, where they form a triangle, all facing the audience. They speak in unison.)

**Fairy, Pilgrim and Wanderer:** 'We speak to the many gods who seem not to care or maybe do not exist. We, human beings, are at the end of our tether. Our planet is nearing the point where it cannot sustain us. We have killed untold numbers of our fellow creatures. All we have left is faith and hope that you will save us. From ourselves. We cannot pray to you anymore. We cannot blame you anymore. We have to surrender the pride that made us blind. Clearly we are being rhetorical. We don't believe in you. We are declaring independence, even with heavy hearts. We shall miss you all, in a way. Not much, though. You have done your worst. Goodbye, gods.'

(Character W detaches from the front trio and stands to the side, still facing the audience. The other two turn to face him. The four characters at the back come forward and stand behind characters F and P, all facing the audience.)

**Mystic Wanderer:** 'I am not sure we knew we were going to say all that. But it is time to end the bullshit once and for all. We are all there is, together with the beauties and horrors of nature. We have to begin taking care of each other and the rest of the living beings. That is our destiny. We have to take care and give love a chance. What else is there but chaos, pain and waste?'

### *Appendix to The Infinite Mountain*

*Note 1. The Scholar-Gipsy by Matthew Arnold is a long poem with three main sections. First, there is the idyllic pastoral landscape, harking back to the Romantic poets. Then there is despair, formulated metaphorically as the bright young scholar who becomes disenchanted with academia (and the sick and inert world as perceived by the poet), and becomes magically involved with the gipsies. The poem ends with a rather odd reference to classicism. It is not a successful poem, especially compared with the short and magisterial 'Dover Beach'. However, Arnold is showing how disjointed is the 19th Century world and how lacking in true spiritual grandeur. There is an interesting analysis of the poem by R.A.Jayantha, University College, Tirupati. He makes the point that Scholar-Gipsy is a quest poem, an epic attempt to repudiate the falseness of society and find true meaning.*

*Note 2. Jude the Obscure, the Thomas Hardy novel is a more down to earth lament not dissimilar to the Arnold poem in that it shows how the fragile craft of a gifted and well-meaning young man can founder on society's rocks. Although not mentioned in the play, Aschenbach's Parzival, gives another, mediaeval version, in which a callow but beautiful and physically powerful youth becomes a wandering assassin in red armour, who is eventually 'saved' by discovering his hidden spirituality.*

*Note 3. Glanvill was a 17th century cleric who, while devoted to the spiritual message of Anglicanism, was hostile to ecclesiastical procedural flummery. His movement, Latitudinarianism, was also characterised by respect for rational thought. This accorded with Arnold's mindset, as it might with the ideas of the agnostic wing of Unitarianism, where intellectual rigour is highly valued.*

*Note 4. The British Humanist Association seems devoid of spiritual awareness or interest, for all its merits as a bulwark against delusional dogma. Hence this attempt to define a non-religious spiritual content that would enhance, even transform, Humanism.*

## Essay 21
## The Everyday Sin of Martyrdom

Imagine seven people in a room on an afternoon in early November. The sun is getting tired of shining outside. A cat plays outside in the conservatory and occasionally his mews can be heard as he voices his displeasure at not being in the human group. He would control it effortlessly and his entrance must be resisted. It is a serious discussion.

**Thesis: Unavoidable Victimhood.**

The woman, **K**, is distressed. She behaves brightly and smiles a lot, but the other six sense her distress. She needs to talk. She talks: The persons in her life who cause her stress are her mother, her sister and her live-in boyfriend. Together they form a nexus of coercion and pain around **K**, who has told the group much of this in the recent past. Her situation isn't getting any better. Mother is old and frail and cannot be left on her own. Sister is presented as selfish and self-seeking, with a keen eye for her finances. Boyfriend is married, with children, and is much-loved by **K** but he is a financial burden to her because of his other commitments. The group listening to **K** don't know the people troubling her and so are unable to see the problem from all sides. **K** has spent some years protecting her mother and feels unable to carry this burden by herself any longer. Sister doesn't help. **K** is trying to establish a new regime in which her mother is safe and her sister does her share and boy-friend is not obliged to worry and slave any more that he does already. How can this be achieved? Not easily? If at all? **K** describes it as a situation in which she has had no alternative but to suffer worry, work and financial loss and she wants more from her life than this mixture of misery. But she is the only one who will carry the burden and if she stops doing it her mother will suffer badly and probably expire rapidly and unpleasantly. Three other members of the group of seven, **S, M,** and **L** become restive. They, two men and one woman, are sympathetic but unconvinced by **K**'s account and conclusions. Before they can develop their arguments, a second man, **V**, tells the group how similarly his mother has suffered. It is, indeed, a broadly similar story. **V**'s mother, a similar age to **S** or **M** (plus/minus seventy) has looked after *her* mother for decades. That has now been changed by the death of the mother. But the siblings have allegedly behaved scandalously and now want financial rewards (for negative behaviour). Her husband is a long-term valetudinarian and **V**'s mother has had to look after him as well as her mother. The opportunity arises in the group of seven for **V**'s partner, **C**, to tell her story, another variant of the victimstate, in which her mother, who recently died in her early sixties, has been parasitised by a live-in boyfriend with a 'weak and self-serving disposition' (to paraphrase **C**'s colourful description of him). **C** has inherited him as a problem, which she is urgently seeking to resolve.

### Key feature of Thesis

Apart from the passion of the accounts, which is acknowledged with sympathy, the three 'sceptics', **S, M,** and **L**, fix upon the repeated use of the phrase 'there is no alternative' to describe the situation involving the people who suffer the burden of care without help. The two sceptical men have both been treated for heart-trouble and the sceptical woman has just lost her husband in his mid-sixties. These are not complacent people, and they are very 'acquainted with grief'. If anything, they are stoical rather than smug, and they seek to help others at every opportunity. The issue for them is the presumed lack of choice. There is, they assert, always choice. The choice is often hard and complex, but it is still choice. They suggest that the idea of non-choice is actually self-condemning and harmful to all concerned, including the unfortunate sufferer at the centre of domestic drama, e.g. each of the three mothers in the stories.

The trio of sceptics meet some strong language from the victim-carers:

'Would you be so fxxxxxg 'cold-blooded' as to let an old lady die in misery?' 'Oh bxxxxr off; if no-one else will help, how could you stand aside?' 'The moral dilemma cannot be bloody ignored: someone has *got to* shoulder the fxxxxxg burden.' 'So you have to get the fxxk on with it however hard it may be.'

### Antithesis

'Yes', say the trio of sceptics, 'These are impressive pressures. But the situations are being misrepresented. There is an artificially single consequential line being drawn. It is hard to see the truth.'

(At the bleakest, as **M** is foolhardy enough to point out,): 'Death of the old women, for example, is not an unnatural consequence of becoming old, sick and frail. It could be seen as an ideal solution, as it usually is in the case of beloved pets. We may be culturally/legally inhibited from affectionate murder, but it is still, at least theoretically, another option. People have been known to go out into the snow and sleep into oblivion.'

Another suggestion was offered: 'What is better, perhaps, is to use all available powers to make everyone share the burden of care. Why would anyone see himself or herself as the only one who can do the job? What is the humanity of sacrificing oneself without extensive examination of the actual choices?'

(There is no meeting of minds. Even **E,** the oldest person in the group, known for her wisdom and stoicism, is irritated by the 'dogmatic' position maintained by the sceptics. This is a serious paradox for the group, when strong scepticism is experienced as 'dogmatic'. In fact, everyone is being dogmatic, or at least emphatic; strong feelings are aroused.)

Eventually, the real but previously hidden reason for the squabble is realised by **S** and his two fellow-sceptics:

'We have failed to make the case for scrupulous self-examination. The fervent victim-carers have therefore got away with an over-simplification plus a personal obfuscation. Their case is unexamined (as Socrates, via Plato, said; "An unexamined life is not worth living").'

Time is now given to examining both sides of the question in the room.

First, a principle has to be established: whose life are you living, your own or someone else's life? If it is not your life, why have you decided to abandon responsibility for it? Can you justify living someone else's life rather than your own?

In other words, the 'sceptics' claimed that the 'carer-victims' were morally and psychologically failing their human heritage. They argued thus:

'Let us postulate that you have already, in your heart or mind, resolutely committed yourself to living your own life. This matter is, say, settled. You are fully and wilfully determined not to do anything that gets in the way of your responsibility to live your own life.

'Now, there is someone in your life, someone you love, a dearest friend, a person who is in a state of travail, perhaps senile, maybe mad, disabled, without a friend or helper in the world. Clearly your commitment to your own life precludes you from taking over the sad life of the person you love. Are you therefore frozen in a state of inaction and remorse? Do you think that your only alternatives are

1. to break your absolute promise to yourself, which is akin to suicide, or,

2. to let the loved and wrecked person lie and rot, which is akin to murder?

'Are you really this naive and lacking in resources? Can't you see that you are 'playing God', being the great ultimate rescuer in the sky? Where is your ego in all this? Do you (secretly?) feel elevated to sainthood or angelhood by your sacrifice? Do you (secretly?) expect that people will worship you for your goodness? Or are you just loving the power of ownership of another poor soul?

'Worse still, how far are you prepared to push others into a conspiracy of pity, with yourself centre-stage?'

The carer-victims, stung by this unexpected rebuke, fight back. Their main argument is the 'selfishness' of the sceptics. So, what is this selfishness, compared with their own 'selflessness'? They claim that the sceptics are ducking their moral responsibility. Yet it is hard to demonstrate.

It is a hard one to argue, too, because each of these sceptics lives a caring and ethical life. They are only guilty of not sacrificing themselves completely.

Without a synthesis there will be no peace in this group.

### Synthesis

The sceptics offer a logical olive-branch. They say this: 'Forget the "no-alternative" story and focus on your own state of being. Try to decide what you really want in your life. At its simplest, maybe you really want to sacrifice yourself for a cause which happens to be another human being. Maybe this is your karma, your fulfilment, or your purpose. If so, why would you complain? Why have we had these aggrieved monologues if you really want martyrdom. You should be happy with what you have chosen, as it is your primary desire. Why blame others? Why not thank them for giving you a clear field?

'This is all about who you are. You *are a belief-system embedded in the workings of your personality.* In Enneagram terms, for example, where the essence of each person is warped and displaced by various societal and personal pressures, the personality, in the shape of mental and emotional fixations, immense energy is diverted to these acquired functions regardless of their origin or value. Usually, there is some tension between what your essence offers and your personality desires. In psychological circles this is called projection, or introjection, and is seen as a cause of neurosis, i.e. conflict of opposing drives.

'We, the sceptics, are not condemning your devotion to care nor the refusal to care by your family members. What we really condemn is a lie, a pretence deep in your motivation. It is sad if you cannot be simply and entirely given over to caring if that is your deeper drive, and conversely it is a crime against yourself if you do the caring and feel resentful.'

The angry carers respond with a mixture of increased indignation and a new uncertainty. They hate the 'condescension' of the sceptics, and the way in which they claim superior understanding. They reply:

'That's all very well, but you are still evading the fundamental issue. If someone is sick or disabled, help is necessary. Who is going to do it? Especially, who is going to do it in a loving and effective way? It costs thousands to have a place in a good nursing home, and the more extensive the care the higher the price. Who is going to pay it if there's no acceptable or accepting family member or friend to do the work?

'Can't you see that "no alternative" scenarios do exist? No alternative, that is, to help from the least selfish, or most good-hearted, friend or relative? It is actually true that a carer has to step in even if they don't want to. It is that "has to" that causes the resentment and it is a fair and understandable reaction.'

On the other hand, they admit, perhaps some self-dishonesty might be operating. There may be a case for closer examination of one's overall mental and emotional balance in an attempt to calm the fury of resentment. They concede, too, that motives are often hidden. After all, the unconscious mind is supposed to be greater in size and power than the conscious mind.

**Synergy** (M's further thoughts after the meeting)

Synthesis offers avenues of agreement, but problems remain unsolved without changes in the psychic energy and ideas involved. The group is unsure how to proceed with this difficult subject. A new initiative is required, one involving creative co-operation within this group and beyond it. How could the issue of self-sacrifice be examined and some new way forward be found?

Human nature, Nature generally, is not very open-minded nor open-handed. The widespread habit of regarding some deity as super-natural doesn't help, because the said deity becomes the excuse for fixed human behaviours and puts back the possibility of progressive change.

No-one in the group of seven appears to suffer from this retrogressive syndrome, yet there are non-rational surges here and there: no-one is proof to superstition of some kind. In a sense, the abhorrence expressed at allowing or assisting death in dire suffering has a supernatural edge to it. Suicide is not generally liked and the small group is not strongly approving of it in any situation. (In this ironic world of ours, what is considered essential kindness to a sick cat, dog, or horse, is deemed a crime for humans. Do we love animals more than the human variety?)

What could the group do? Is there a **synergic** rationale available but so far unrecognised? They have had the antagonistic skirmish, they have started to see something in the opposite viewpoint, so could they step forward to a new position?

**Isn't this our real task?**

www.ingramcontent.com/pod-product-compliance
Lightning Source LLC
Chambersburg PA
CBHW060847280326
41934CB00007B/955